MARK O'ROWE

Mark O'Rowe began writing in 1994. His first play, *The Aspidistra Code*, received a rehearsed reading at the Peacock Theatre, Dublin. The second, *From Both Hips*, was produced by Fishamble and won the Stewart Parker BBC radio drama award. His third play, *Howie the Rookie*, was produced by the Bush Theatre, London, transferring to Dublin and Edinburgh. It won the 1999 George Devine Award and the 1999 Rooney Prize for Irish Literature.

He lives in Dublin.

EX LIBRIS

BOOKS
BY THE
RIVER

@BOOKSBYTHESEAANDRIVER

Mark O'Rowe

FROM BOTH HIPS
Two Plays

From Both Hips
&
The Aspidistra Code

NICK HERN BOOKS
London

A Nick Hern Book

From Both Hips: Two Plays first published in Great Britain
in 1999 as a paperback original by Nick Hern Books Limited,
14 Larden Road, London W3 7ST

From Both Hips copyright © 1999, Mark O'Rowe
The Aspidistra Code copyright © 1999, Mark O'Rowe

Mark O'Rowe has asserted his right to be identified as the
author of this work

Typeset by Country Setting, Kingsdown, Kent CT14 8ES
Printed and bound in Great Britain by Athenaeum Press,
Gateshead

ISBN 1-85459-445-1

A CIP catalogue record for this book is available from
the British Library

Contents

FROM BOTH HIPS

From Both Hips was originally produced at the Little Theatre, Tallaght, transferring to the Project Arts Centre, Dublin and the Tron Theatre, Glasgow, produced by Fishamble. The cast was as follows:

PAUL	Ger Carey
WILLY	Sean Rocks
LIZ	Marion O'Dwyer
ADELE	Clodagh O'Donoghue
THERESA	Fionnuala Murphy
IRENE	Catherine Walsh

Directed by Jim Culleton
Designed by Blaíthín Sheerin
Lighting by Nick McCall

Characters

LIZ

ADELE

PAUL

THERESA

WILLY

IRENE

ACT ONE

Scene One

A sitting room in a normal, working-class house. Stage left, the hallway to the front door. Up right, the door to the sitting room. Up left, stairs leading off. A table and chairs. A sofa. LIZ sits on the sofa reading the paper. ADELE stands in the centre of the room, looking around. She exits. She returns. She exits again.

LIZ. Adele! (*Calling.*) Adele! What are you doing? C'mere!

ADELE (*entering, just inside door to kitchen*). What?

LIZ. See what it says here?

ADELE. What? (*Exits.*)

LIZ (*calling*). Where are you going? Will you stop going in and out? Come back in, will you?

ADELE (*off-stage*). What?

LIZ. Come back in and sit down.

    ADELE *enters and stands there.*

    What are you doing?

ADELE. I'm looking for the ship.

LIZ. Well, just ask me. It's inside on top of the press. It's grand. Sit down.

ADELE. No, I'll stand. What does it say?

LIZ. It says . . . You're making me very nervous, there.

ADELE. Good. Go on. Read. Tell me.

LIZ. Something I never knew. Something very surprising. Dogs . . .

ADELE. Mmm?

LIZ. . . . Dogs. Right here, some professor. Dogs are incapable of love.

ADELE. Dogs?

LIZ. . . . Some professor, here. Although they appear, he says, loving and affectionate, they actually don't have any emotions. It's all . . . The way they act, their behaviour. It's all instinctual.

ADELE. Yeah?

LIZ. That's not really fair, is it?

ADELE. Why not?

LIZ. Well, love's a two way street. I wouldn't want to be giving love to something if it wasn't going to love me back. (*Pause.*)

ADELE. Mmm.

LIZ. You know?

ADELE. Were you thinking of buying a dog?

LIZ. No, no, God!

ADELE. Well, then.

LIZ. But I know people who have dogs. Ciara and Joe have one, and thing . . . Theresa Nolan. She's fairly into her dog, actually. She comes out sometimes, she reeks of it, you can smell it off her clothes and all.

ADELE. Reeks?

LIZ. Bits of brown hairs on her jumper. Yeah, reeks. Ah, I'm a bit addled now, damn!

ADELE *sits down and lights a cigarette.*

ADELE. What's wrong?

LIZ. I feel like I should do something about it.

ADELE. Do some . . . What?

LIZ. I feel like I should tell them.

ADELE. Who? Theresa Nolan?

LIZ. She's fairly into her dog. Ciara and Joe . . . Who else do
    I . . .?

ADELE. Tell them what? That their dogs don't love them?

LIZ. Yeah. They should know.

ADELE. Ah, Liz.

LIZ. If I don't tell them, they could go on through life living a
    lie. Their dogs don't love them, even though they love their
    dogs. That's a lie, they're being cheated, they should be
    told. On the other hand . . .

ADELE. On the other hand, ignorance, Liz.

LIZ. What about it?

ADELE. Ignorance is bliss.

LIZ. It's ignorance, Adele. Nothing good comes of it. I'm
    saying if I tell, it'll hurt. It'll hurt at first.

ADELE. Could.

LIZ. Nobody likes being told they're in an unrequited
    relationship.

ADELE. You wouldn't call it a relationship. (*Pause.*)

LIZ. Are they communicating, Adele?

ADELE. I don't . . .

LIZ. In some way, a dog and its master, mistress. Its owner.
    Are they, like, aware of each other?

ADELE. I suppose.

LIZ. Well, then they're communicating. It's happening over a
    period of time, then it's a relationship. There's physical
    contact going on? Yes. In Theresa Nolan's case, a lot,
    judging from the stink on her, then it's a close relationship.
    Jesus! She feels love, the dog feels nothing, she's being
    made a fool of. Her dog's working the dark trick on her.

ADELE. The what?

LIZ. The dark trick. And she's not the type of girl who has many friends. It's probably the best friend she has. She's playing the fool for her dog and she doesn't even know it, she thinks it's two sided and . . . You all right? (ADELE *is distant.*) . . . She's getting nothing in return. Are you all right? (*Beat.*)

ADELE. Hmm? (*Beat.*) Yeah. I'm just . . . I'm kinda . . . I'm like . . . Just give me two minutes.

LIZ. Are you sure?

ADELE (*flustered*). No, no. Just gimme . . . I have to get my head . . .

LIZ. Okay.

ADELE. . . . Just two minutes, give me.

LIZ. Okay. You sure? Do you want me to get something for you?

ADELE. Yeah. No. I'm fine. It's just . . . Okay. All right. That's it.

LIZ. I'm say . . .

ADELE. Go on. Tell me the rest.

LIZ. I'm saying . . . You all right?

ADELE. Sorry. Yeah. My mind was just . . . This way, that, up, million directions. Go on.

LIZ. It's all right . . . Well . . . For some people, you love someone and they don't love you. But they *like* you. Some people can live with that. That's enough for them. Least there's some emotion going on, okay? But a dog . . . doesn't . . . feel . . . anything. What do you think?

ADELE. Well, are you sure it's true?

LIZ. It says it right here in the Echo, Adele.

ADELE. But, that doesn't make it . . .

LIZ (*interrupting. Getting up*). I'm gonna ring Theresa. To hell with the other two, Ciara and . . . They've got each other, anyway.

ADELE. You're gonna ring, what are you gonna do?

LIZ. I'm gonna ring Theresa.

> LIZ *picks up the phone and dials.* ADELE *puts her cigarette out.*

LIZ (*into phone*). Hello? Theresa. How are you? It's . . . Who d'you think it is? It's Liz. Yeah, how's it going?

> ADELE *exits to the kitchen.*

Listen. What are you doing? Nothing. Good. Come over to Adele's house, will you? (*Pause.*) Because . . . Just come over and you'll find out. I need to tell you something. That doesn't . . . (*Pause.*) That's no excuse, you just told me you weren't doing anything, so come on. Half an hour or so. All right? (*Pause.*) Bit of company since you're bored. (*Pause.*) Yes, it is important. Yep. Okay. See you then.

LIZ (*calling to kitchen*). I told her to drop down. (*Pause. Calling.*) Adele!

> ADELE *enters with a glass of water and a pill. She takes the pill, chases it with some water.*

Should you be taking that now?

ADELE. Just the one.

LIZ. You only took one a while ago, Adele.

ADELE. It's just the one, Liz.

LIZ. I wasn't comfortable about breaking it to her over the phone, so I asked her to drop down. (*Pause.*)

ADELE. The dog?

LIZ. Rather in person. So if she needs a hug or something. She might need a . . .

ADELE. You're gonna tell her her dog doesn't love her?!

LIZ. I couldn't do it over the phone, she's on her own there. She might need a bit of support, a hug, some comforting words, someone to listen and help, to tell her . . .

ADELE. But, what about . . . ?

LIZ. . . . everything's . . .

ADELE. . . . you shouldn't . . .

LIZ. . . . everything's going to be all right. To calm down, to . . .

ADELE. What about . . .?

LIZ. To pull yourself together. (*Pause.*)

ADELE. What about Paul? (*Beat.*)

LIZ. We'll *be* here.

ADELE. *And* Theresa?

LIZ. The more, the merrier, a bigger welcome, Adele.

ADELE. He's only expecting you and me.

LIZ. He'll be delighted to see her. Paul's fond of Theresa, he'll be delighted.

ADELE. But, he's only expecting . . .

LIZ. Yeah! So, that's . . . That'll be the surprise. Paul'll come home and there'll be three of us here to see him instead of two, a bigger welcome, the more, the merrier.

ADELE. He might want some peace and quiet.

LIZ. And if he does, we'll give it to him. *After* we welcome him and he sees he's got friends. Theresa has to be told.

ADELE *exits with glass of water to the kitchen.*

(*Calling.*) Sooner the better she finds out she's being tricked.

Pause. ADELE *returns, lights another cigarette.*

ADELE. You should have met her somewhere else.

LIZ. I thought of that, but I want us to be here, the more, the merrier, three's a crowd, but four's a party.

ADELE. He might not want a party.

LIZ. Just for when he comes in. He can hang around and chat for an hour, have a brandy and do what . . .? Head off to bed or watch telly or . . .

ADELE. 'Cos he might want to.

LIZ. You give us the signal and we'll head off. Say 'Geronimo.'

ADELE. Geronimo?

LIZ. That's the password. Say 'Geronimo' and I'll take that as my cue.

ADELE. See, we shouldn't . . . Paul's . . . We shouldn't . . .

LIZ. I know.

ADELE. . . . He's . . .

LIZ. . . . We'll head off. If he wants us to head off . . .

ADELE. . . . You'll . . .

LIZ. . . . We'll go up to the pub.

ADELE. That might be best.

LIZ. Yeah. You haven't been alone together for more than five minutes in ages. Be nice for you to get re-acquainted. You can have an early night. Go to bed. Make the beast with two backs.

ADELE. Liz!

LIZ. The *beautiful* beast with two backs.

ADELE (*embarrassed*). We'll be . . . We won't be . . .

LIZ. The beautiful beast of true love . . .

ADELE. . . . Stop, Liz.

LIZ (*pause*) . . . with two backs.

ADELE. Liz! (*Pause.*)

LIZ. Are you looking forward? (*Pause.* ADELE *looks distant.*) Adele.

ADELE. What?

LIZ. Are you looking forward? Are you all right?

ADELE. I'm anxious.

LIZ. Did I upset you, there?

ADELE. No, I'm just anxious.

LIZ. Where's his present? Bring it in, put it on the table, so he can see it when he comes in. He'll say, 'Whose is that?' And you'll say, 'It's yours.' (*Pause.* ADELE *looks distant.*)

ADELE. Yeah.

LIZ. Go on. It's on top of the press. Go.

ADELE. Yeah.

LIZ. Go and get it.

> ADELE *exits and returns with a model ship. Unmade. Still in its box.*

Put it there on the table.

She does.

No. Like this. (*Repositions box.*) So he can see the name of it and all. Lovely. (*Pause.*) Has he ever done one before?

ADELE. Not since I've known him. Wait . . . Lemme . . . Before, may . . .? Just thinking . . .

LIZ. No?

ADELE. Has he . . .?

LIZ. No? No?

ADELE. I don't think so.

LIZ. Good. No? Good. It's a good choice. Something to pass the time.

ADELE. Was a good idea.

LIZ. It is. (*Of model.*) Did you ever?

ADELE. Never.

LIZ. I heard that fifty percent of those things never get finished. Fifty percent.

ADELE. Fifty?!

LIZ. Half of them. Of every one of those things that gets bought. So, you'd better warn him.

ADELE. Paul'll finish it.

LIZ. I'm sure he will.

ADELE. He wouldn't start it if he wasn't going to finish it.

LIZ. Yeah.

ADELE. Wouldn't see the point. He'll enjoy that.

LIZ. He will. Something to pass the time. Two weeks?

ADELE. Yeah.

LIZ. Probably *take* him two weeks.

ADELE. And even if it takes longer . . .

LIZ. I know. He'd probably take another few days off.

ADELE. Just to finish it. Yeah. (*Pause.*)

LIZ. Perfect present.

ADELE. Yeah.

> *The telephone rings.* ADELE *answers it. While she's on the phone,* LIZ *goes over to the model ship, turns it on its side, then puts it back the way it was. She looks at the door. Moves the ship forward on the table, so that it'll be in a more advantageous position.*

ADELE. Hello? No, no, he's not in at the moment. Can I . . .? No, yes, I'm sure. (*Pause.*) I don't. If you want to try . . . (*Pause.*) Well, I don't know if . . . (*Pause. She hangs up. Pause.*)

LIZ. What?

ADELE. I don't know.

LIZ. Who?

ADELE. Some man.

LIZ. Who was he?

ADELE. Paul. (*Pause.*) Looking for Paul.

LIZ. For what?

ADELE. Bit sinister.

LIZ. Who? The man?

ADELE. Said he was going to call around. Bit scary.

LIZ. When?

ADELE. Later was all he said. He didn't sound too happy.

LIZ. How'd he sound?

ADELE. Not happy.

LIZ. How?

ADELE. Sinister.

LIZ. Sinister.

ADELE. He didn't tell me anything else. Ah, God!

LIZ. It was probably just a friend of his.

ADELE (*to herself*). Angry, maybe?

LIZ. He sounded angry?

ADELE. Sounded sinister.

LIZ. And you don't know who it was?!

ADELE. No.

LIZ. You sure? You know his friends.

ADELE. No. I don't know this one.

LIZ. Surely . . .

ADELE. Not this one. A scary voice, it was.

LIZ. Sinister.

ADELE. I hope he's not in trouble. (*Pause. She looks distracted.*)

LIZ. You all right?

ADELE. Hmm?

LIZ. What'd he say?

ADELE. Just . . . (*Pause. She looks distracted/ upset.*)

LIZ. What? Adele?

ADELE. Two mi . . . I'm fine. I'm just . . . I'm kinda . . .
(*Pause.*) I wonder.

LIZ. It'll be grand.

ADELE. That's strange. (*Pause.*)

LIZ. Listen, why don't you . . .? That's a bit drab. Why don't
you dress up a bit for him?

ADELE. This?

LIZ. Bit drab, Adele. What about your black trousers I
borrowed on Thursday?

ADELE. Dress up?

LIZ. Impress him even more, and the sexy white cardigan. Just
to give him a real welcome.

ADELE. I . . .

LIZ. Go on.

ADELE. Should . . . The woolly one?

LIZ. He'll love it, go on. Yeah. The woolly white one and the
black trousers.

ADELE. I should dress up for him?

LIZ. He'll love it. A bigger welcome. We'll have the model
there, Theresa'll be here to make up the numbers, the more,
the merrier, a bit of style from you. Go on. It's a statement,
says 'I love you.'

ADELE. Will he know that?

LIZ. 'Course he will. (*Pause.*)

ADELE. Yeah. (*Pause.*)

LIZ. Who'd have thought that, huh? 'Bout the dogs.

ADELE. Mmm.

LIZ. They can't love.

ADELE. Yeah.

LIZ. For their appearance, you'd think they'd a ton of love.
   Wagging their . . . And their actions. Wagging their little
   tails and snuggling, and licking your face. (*Sighs.*) Instinct.

ADELE. Yeah.

LIZ. It's a shame. I'd say it's gonna be a big disappointment to
   a lot of people with dogs.

The doorbell rings.

Theresa. Get some spirits out, there.

She exits to hall door. We hear it opening. ADELE *exits to
sitting room.*

THERESA. (*off-stage*). How are you, Liz?

LIZ (*off-stage*). Theresa. Come in. Come in. Listen. I'm sorry
   to get you down in such a rush.

   ADELE *returns with a bottle of brandy and glasses. She
   stands in the centre of the room, listening.*

THERESA. (*off-stage*). Is it important?

LIZ (*off-stage*). It is, yeah. Gimme there . . . (*Pause.*) Just hang
   it there. Grand. How are you?

THERESA. (*off-stage*). I'm fine. Is Adele here?

LIZ (*off-stage*). She's inside. How are you?

THERESA. (*off-stage*). I'm fine. What's going on?

LIZ (*off-stage*). I think you'll need to sit down first.

   Silence. ADELE *remains standing. Frozen in the centre of
   the room.*

   Blackout.

Scene Two

A typical sitting room. PAUL *sits on the sofa with a walking stick in his lap.* THERESA *enters with two cups of tea. She gives one to* PAUL.

THERESA. There you go.

> THERESA *sits down.* PAUL *drinks. Winces.*

> All right?

PAUL. Bit hot. (*Blows on it.*)

THERESA. Do you want me to put some more milk in it?

PAUL. No. (*Drinks.*)

THERESA. Good to see you. How's the leg?

PAUL. Crap. It's not my leg, it's my hip.

THERESA. How is it?

PAUL. Crap. (*Pause. Drinks.*)

THERESA. Thanks for calling in, Paul. I was getting to miss you. Getting a bit lonely. How are you?

PAUL. Where's your telly?

THERESA. I was broken into.

PAUL. When?

THERESA. Last night. The telly and the video.

PAUL. You were broken into?!

THERESA. They didn't touch anything else. Just the . . .

PAUL. And where were you?

THERESA. In bed, fast asleep. I didn't hear a thing. Just the telly and the video. They must've known there was somebody upstairs.

PAUL. Broken into. Jesus.

THERESA. I'm scared.

PAUL. The bastards.

THERESA. If they'd've come upstairs . . .

PAUL. Telly and the video.

THERESA. I didn't hear a thing.

PAUL. Did you call the cops?

THERESA. Yeah, I went down this morning.

PAUL. No help, I bet.

THERESA. Nothing. I had to fill in a few forms, but they told me . . .

PAUL. They told you, I bet, the fuckers. They told you there was nothing they could do.

THERESA. I never wrote down the serial number, and even if I had, they'd . . . The robbers would've filed it off by now, some family has a new telly and video. And the worst thing, they said . . .

PAUL. Useless bastards.

THERESA. . . . Worst thing, and it's kind of sad . . .

PAUL. What's that?

THERESA. The people who have it now are probably quite poor, not well off, and they bought it, like, whatsit? Hot. A hot video because they couldn't afford a new one. But they wouldn't be, like, criminals. Just a family trying to get by.

PAUL. They should be strung up.

THERESA. But, they'd be decent otherwise.

PAUL. The coppers.

THERESA. They do their best.

PAUL. They do, all right, the fuckers!

THERESA. Since . . . I've been a nervous wreck all day. I feel . . . Do you know? If someone breaks into your home . . .

PAUL. We've an alarm.

THERESA. If someone breaks in . . .

PAUL (*interrupting. Not listening*). Some of the nurses in
there, Theresa. (*Pause.*)

THERESA. They take good care of you?

PAUL. Excellent. Some nice nurses.

THERESA. Nice?

PAUL. Good looking. Sexy nurses gear. I don't know what it is
about them.

THERESA. Mmm.

PAUL. Some gorgeous looking things. (*Pause.*)

THERESA. I think it's . . . Could be they're taking care of you,
so . . . They're . . . You know, that's what's so attractive
about them. Because they're there just for you and they're
taking care of you. Maybe that's why they're . . . You know?

PAUL. They're fucking gorgeous is what it is. I asked one of
them out this morning. (*Pause.*) I'm meeting her tonight.
(*Pause.*)

THERESA. Did you?

Pause. They look at each other.

PAUL. Just testing you.

THERESA. You didn't?

PAUL. 'Course I didn't.

THERESA. Oh.

PAUL. Testing you, I was.

THERESA. Right.

PAUL. 'Course I didn't.

THERESA. Why?

PAUL. Why?

THERESA. Yeah.

She moves closer and closer as they speak.

PAUL. Because . . . Yeah, they took care of me. Grand. But none of them were my special friend.

THERESA. Your special friend.

PAUL. Yeah.

THERESA. And who's your special friend?

She leans on him.

PAUL. Aagh. Fuck. Get away.

THERESA. Oh, God.

PAUL. Get away. Ouch!

THERESA. Sorry.

PAUL. Fucking hip!

THERESA. I'm sorry.

PAUL. Jesus!

THERESA. Are you all right? I'm sorry, I didn't mean to . . .

PAUL. Fucking hip!

THERESA (*pause*). I'm sorry.

PAUL. You don't take good care of me. (*Pause.*)

THERESA. But I'm your special friend. I want to take care of you. (*Pause.*) Is it bad?

PAUL. It's bad enough. I need this fucking thing, don't I?

He shows the walking stick.

THERESA (*loveydovey speak*). But you have your special friend, now.

PAUL. My special pal.

THERESA. Your special pal who'll help you and who'll look after you.

PAUL. Who'll tend to me, yeah?

THERESA. Who'll tend to you specially.

PAUL. Better than the nurses?

THERESA. Much better. The way only a special . . . (*Kisses him.*) pal . . . (*Kisses him.*) can . . . (*Kisses him.*)

PAUL. Ah, God. Get away.

THERESA. What?

PAUL. Get away, the . . . Wash your face.

THERESA. What?

PAUL. Smell of dog off you.

THERESA. Oh, no.

PAUL. I told you before.

THERESA. I forgot.

PAUL. Wash your face. That's the most unhygienic thing you can do.

THERESA. I can't help it. He likes to lick my face, he likes to be cuddled.

PAUL. You stink of it. Come on. Theresa!

THERESA. I was lo . . . (*Pause.*) Fuck you! Fuck off if you don't like it. (*Pause.*)

PAUL. I don't like it.

THERESA. Well fuck off, then, you're only out of hospital.

PAUL. All I'm asking you is to wash your face.

THERESA. You're not coming into my place and ordering . . . That's the rudest thing. My face isn't smelly. How dare you come in . . . How . . . I was playing with Toby. If you don't like it . . . If . . . Well, fuck off, then, if you don't like it. (*Pause.*)

PAUL. Do you want me to go, then?

THERESA (*realising she's gone too far*). No, I don't wa . . .

PAUL. Head off on my merry way?

THERESA. No, it's just like . . .

PAUL. Say if I was eating garlic . . . I know you don't like garlic.

THERESA. No, I don't.

PAUL. So, if I was eating garlic, you'd ask me to brush my teeth and I wouldn't say no, because I know you don't like it.

THERESA. If you were . . .

PAUL. Garlic. Same thing here. I don't like the smell of dog, it's the exact same thing. (*Pause.*) It's just it's polite, like, it's a bit of consideration.

THERESA. Mmm.

PAUL. The smell or the taste. It's the same thing. I *want* to kiss you.

THERESA. Yeah.

PAUL. I *like* kissing you, but . . .

THERESA. I know. (*Pause.*)

PAUL. Go on.

She exits. PAUL *gets up slowly.*

I'm gonna make a phone call. Is that all right?

THERESA (*off-stage. Calling. Loveydovey*). Only if you're still my special pal.

PAUL. You know I am.

He makes a face, takes out a piece of paper and dials a number.

Know who this is? Is . . . ? No. Put him on. *Him.* You know who. Put him on. (*Pause.*) Yeah, fuckface, how are you? (*Pause.*) Yeah. I just got out, so this is where it begins, do you hear me? (*Pause.*) Well, I'm sorry. I'm sorry, but, you know . . . (*Pause.*) That's your problem. We all have stuff to deal with. (*Pause.*) My heart bleeds. (*Pause.*) Listen. You listening? Right. Carefully, now. Fuck her and fuck you.

Fuck the pair of you. I'm out and the wheel is in motion. Do you hear me? The wheel is turning.

He hangs up and limps back over to the sofa. He eases himself down painfully, takes a sip of his tea. Enter THERESA.

THERESA. All done.

PAUL. Good. Are you gonna get a new telly?

THERESA. Suppose I'll have to.

PAUL. Good.

THERESA. Who were you ringing? Adele?

PAUL. No. The bloke.

THERESA. What did you say?

PAUL. I told him the cogs are spinning. Don't say anything, Theresa. Don't open your trap, I don't give a shite.

THERESA. Don't talk to me li . . .

PAUL. I don't give a flying fuck, that's where the line is drawn. Anyone who has any objections . . . Anyone who has . . . They can . . . Look at me. (*Pause.*) Theresa.

THERESA. What are you going to say?

PAUL. In the papers, the Echo?

THERESA. Yeah.

PAUL. That's not for your ears. You'll find out when you read it.

THERESA. Tell me.

PAUL. It's a surprise. Tony Kelly's column. You'll see it when you read it. Look at me.

THERESA. What?

PAUL. Look at me. I want you on my side. This is just so he knows what he's let himself in for. Do you know I can't even sign on? I've another two weeks before I can go back to work.

THERESA. But you're going to get compensation.

PAUL. I don't care. I don't give a fuck. I want *him* to pay. Those fuckers think they're all powerful. I'll show him it can be personal sometimes.

THERESA. Doesn't mean you have to harass him. You're making whatchamicallit telephone calls.

PAUL. I'll show the fucker. I'm gonna, in a few years, when I'm older, I'll be one of those poor fuckers who can't walk when it rains.

THERESA. You won't.

PAUL. 'Course I will. A bum hip.

THERESA. Bum?

PAUL. A bum hip. A hip that 'plays up' when it rains. And it always fucking rains. Ever hear the phrase 'An old war wound?' That's what it'll be like. And it'll be 'Playing up.' I'll be a, what's the word?

THERESA. Infirm?

PAUL. Fucking retard's what I'll be. (*Pause.*)

THERESA. Your old war wound.

PAUL. Yeah.

THERESA. I think that's romantic.

PAUL. You would. (*Pause.*)

THERESA. How long are you staying? Do you've to . . .?

PAUL. Adele? No. After.

THERESA. Oh.

PAUL. I'm dreading going home. (*She looks at him.*) But I'm not staying here. I'm going for a drink. I've a few things to sort out.

THERESA. Who are you going with?

PAUL. On my own. I need to be on my own for a few hours. Away from nurses and doctors and . . . I've plans to make.

I'm gonna be busy for a while. Preparing and planning. Did you wash your face?

THERESA. Yep.

PAUL. C'mere. (*She approaches.*) Be careful, now.

They kiss.

THERESA. Let's go upstairs.

PAUL. I can't.

THERESA. A quickie.

PAUL. I can't.

THERESA. Why not?

PAUL. 'Cos of this. I can't with this.

THERESA. Try.

PAUL. What do you mean try? I can't. Next few weeks, now, I'll be impotent.

THERESA. Not impotent.

PAUL. Yes, impotent. Technically, I'm impotent. I'm an impotent man. A man whose manhood doesn't work.

THERESA. For the next couple of weeks.

PAUL. Yeah. For the next couple of weeks. It still gets to me. I'm proud of my cocksmanship.

THERESA. And so you should be.

PAUL. And I like to use it. Not that it's my cock that doesn't work. It's my hip. I can't move. There's nothing wrong with my virility.

THERESA. Sure, don't I know.

PAUL. It's just my hip.

THERESA. I know. (*Pause.*) Is she expecting you?

PAUL. Who?

THERESA. Adele.

PAUL. She's got her sister over there.

THERESA. Liz?

PAUL. They can keep each other company. One of them's bad enough. Adele's hard to take these days.

THERESA. You'd think she'd be a bit more . . . capable nowadays.

PAUL. I'm doing the best I can.

THERESA. I'm sure you are.

PAUL. But, when you can't even talk to your wife properly . . .

THERESA. I know.

PAUL. And, now, since this thing . . . (*Holds up stick.*) I'm doing my best.

THERESA. I know you are. (*She hugs him.*)

PAUL. Watchit. Watchit.

THERESA. Sorry.

PAUL. Anyway, different things affect different people in different ways. Nah, I'm gonna go for a drink, do some thinking.

THERESA. Right. (*Pause.*)

PAUL. We must be the unluckiest people in the world.

THERESA. You're lucky you've got me around.

Pause. He looks at her.

PAUL. What the fuck is that supposed to mean? I'm lucky . . .?

THERESA. No. It just means . . .

PAUL. I'm lucky I've got . . . I should be . . .

THERESA. . . . That's not . . .

PAUL. . . . I should be grateful to you?

THERESA. No.

PAUL. . . . That you're around?

THERESA. That's not what I meant. Stop. I was messing. Jesus! It's good that we can . . .

PAUL. That we can what?

THERESA. That we can have a good time together. That's all I was saying. It was a joke.

PAUL. Last thing I need's bloody jokes. (*Pause.*) Some of the nurses in that hospital, though. (*Pause.*)

THERESA. I'm a bit, Paul.

PAUL. What?

THERESA. I'm a bit scared. Over this burglary.

PAUL. What burglary?

THERESA. The telly and the video. I feel . . .

PAUL. Oh, *your* burglary. Why?

THERESA. In case they come back. What's the word?

PAUL. Why would they?

THERESA. Whatsit? I feel . . .

PAUL. There's nothing to take.

THERESA. Very funny.

PAUL. Maybe *you* should be grateful that *I'm* around. (*Pause.*) Yeah. That's what I'll do. I'm gonna . . . You know Kevin? Tony Kelly's a friend of his, said he'd be interested. You know Tony Kelly?

THERESA. Is he the cri . . .?

PAUL. The crime correspondent, yeah. Genius way with words, he has. Kevin said he'd be interested in my version of events. Get in there now, I'm gonna talk about incompetency, I'm gonna talk about someone who doesn't do his job properly, who shouldn't *be* doing that job, who shouldn't've been doing it in the first place. Detailed description of events, and then I'll drop the bomb. (*Imitates the sound of an explosion.*) The laughing stock of the country. He won't be able to show his face for a year.

THERESA. What *is* the bomb?

PAUL. None of your business. You can read about it in the Echo.

He raises himself from a sitting to standing position with the aid of his walking stick and a loud grunt.

Jesus! (*Beat.*) Shite! Gimme, have you . . .? Pen and paper. Just a piece of paper. I'll have to make some notes.

THERESA. A piece of . . .

PAUL. Yeah. Pen and a piece of paper. Have you got it?

THERESA. Yeah. Hang on. (*She exits.*)

PAUL (*calling*). I'll go up and make some notes, I think it's better to write stuff down.

THERESA (*off-stage*). Will a pencil do?

PAUL. Have you no pens? (*Pause.*)

THERESA (*off-stage*). No. (*She returns.*)

PAUL. Right. Just gimme the pencil.

THERESA. And there's your paper.

PAUL. Nice one. Right.

He turns towards the door.

THERESA. You going?

PAUL. Yeah.

THERESA. Have another cup of tea.

PAUL. Booze, I need.

THERESA. I've got wine and . . .

PAUL. . . . A pint. From the pumps. Haven't had a pint in . . .

THERESA. Hang on here for a while.

PAUL. I can't.

THERESA. Well, can I come with you?

PAUL. No. What did . . .? Wasn't I just saying? I've to make notes, I've to be on my own, I've to get my head together.

THERESA. Well, I'll come up, have the one . . . a glass, and then I'll leave.

PAUL. Sorry, Theresa. No. Bit of solitude, gimme . . . (*He kisses her.*) Have to go. (*He hobbles towards the door.*) Give you a ring tomorrow, all right?

THERESA. What time?

PAUL. Some stage during the day. (*She opens the door for him.*)

THERESA. All right. (*He kisses her.*)

PAUL. Or the evening. See you.

The telephone rings. THERESA *jumps nervously.*

THERESA. Paul!

PAUL. What?

THERESA. Hang on a sec', will you?

PAUL (*impatient*). Come on!

THERESA. Just 'til I . . . (*Points at phone.*)

PAUL. Think it's the fuckin' burglars or somethin'?

She answers the phone. PAUL *waits at the door.*

THERESA. Hello? Who is this? (*Pause.*) Oh. (*Pause.*) Nothing. (*Pause.*) Why? (*Beat.*) What, though? I'm a bit tired. (*Pause.*) But, what? (*Beat.*) I'm fairly tired. (*Pause.*) Is it important? (*Beat.*) All right. Yeah. Yeah. Yeah. Okay, see you.

PAUL. Who's that?

THERESA. Oh, it's just . . . A . . . Just this . . .

PAUL. You cheating on me, Theresa?

THERESA. No. It's a girl I know, wants me to . . .

PAUL. Some bloke, yeah?

THERESA. A woman. A girlfriend.

PAUL. Bit on the side?

THERESA. Paul!

PAUL. I'm testin'. Am I allowed go now?

THERESA. Yeah.

PAUL. Good.

THERESA. Thanks.

PAUL. You're welcome.

THERESA. You okay?

PAUL. Yeah.

THERESA. You sure?

PAUL. I'm crippled and I'm impotent. I'm grand. See you.

THERESA. See you.

He exits.

THERESA *stands silently.*

Blackout.

Scene Three

Another sitting room. IRENE *sits on her sofa.* WILLY *paces behind her.*

IRENE. Well?

WILLY. Mmm.

IRENE. Willy.

He sighs.

IRENE. What was he like?

WILLY. Like on telly. He listens, sits there in his chair, he says 'hmm', and 'go on', and treats you like a fucking child.

IRENE *looks at him.*

Like a . . . Sorry. You'd end up believing you were a six year old. Where's Tommo?

IRENE. He's in bed. If we decide to, Sandra said she'd come over and babysit, no problem. If we want to go out. I thought you might . . . If you'd like to go out.

WILLY. God!

IRENE. Yeah?

WILLY. Terrible.

IRENE. C'mon, hardshaw. You'll get used to it.

WILLY. Yeah. We can get used to anything, can't we. Doesn't mean that everything you get used to is good for you. There've been people found up the mountains in Canada've got used to eating dirty roots and smearing themselves in shite to keep warm. They've gotten used to it, but it doesn't mean it's good that they've gotten used to it.

IRENE. That's horrible.

WILLY. That's what they do, Irene.

IRENE. What did he say?

He lights a cigarette.

WILLY. They'd probably consider *us* uncivilised.

IRENE. What did he say?

WILLY. He asked me . . . (*Takes a pull. Exhales.*) He asked me what kind of things I was afraid of. He asked me about my history, he asked me about you, about my relationship with little Tommo, about . . . Listen to this. About whether I ever get angry at him.

IRENE. He's trying to cure you.

WILLY. About whether I ever get angry at my son. There's nothing wrong with me, Irene. There's nothing wrong with me. They're testing me, the bastards, and guess what? Guess what? I'm failing. Treating me like a child. Talk about humiliation. He asked me about that day . . .

IRENE. You weren't humiliated.

WILLY. I was humiliated. Grown ups don't talk to each other like that. Grown ups talk to each other like adults. We don't tell each other everything's going to be all right. We talk about adult things. We converse.

IRENE. He's your doctor.

WILLY. There's nothing wrong with me. You'd wanna hear the bloke. Talks with, you know that accent, it's Irish, but it sounds kind of English. Very . . . Very . . .

IRENE. Yeah.

WILLY. Kind of a newsreader accent, what the newsreaders have. Middle of the whatcha . . . session, his wife rings up, think it was his wife. All of a sudden, he's speaking like anyone else.

IRENE. His professional manner.

WILLY. Like you or me.

IRENE. Right.

WILLY. Hangs up the phone and all of a sudden, he's on the telly again, reading the news. Talking like I'm a baby, asking stupid things.

IRENE. But there's things they probably need to clear up.

WILLY. Yeah. To clear up. Like how incompetent I was, how much stress I was under, like . . . Do . . . He actually asked me do I suffer from stress or nervousness? In general life, like. I'm the most relaxed man in the world. I only get worked up when . . . you know . . . (*Takes a pull. Exhales.*) something deserves getting worked up over.

IRENE. Well, he obviously doesn't know you yet.

WILLY. And the accent. Don't forget the accent, disappears when he's on the phone. Trying to determine my mental state.

IRENE. Your mental state's fine.

WILLY. My career.

IRENE. I know.

WILLY. I'll be . . .

IRENE. Everything'll be okay, Willy.

WILLY. And this fucker, this other fella. I don't know what I'm going to do. It was an accident.

IRENE. Well, he can't be much of a human being . . .

WILLY. An accident.

IRENE. . . . He can't . . . If he can't see that.

WILLY. What to do, what to do? I'm gonna be thrown out, I know it.

IRENE. We'll see.

WILLY. I'll get the sack. Wait'll you see. The lads were all acting different in the station today.

IRENE. I'm sure they're all rooting for you, Willy.

WILLY. It's a joke. *I'm* a bloody joke. Promoted for two weeks. Two weeks and I screw up. My fifteen minutes of respect.

IRENE. Everyone respects you.

WILLY. I . . . This psychia . . . psychologist, whatever he is, I asked him, what about this bloke? Could he be, like, a big threat, because, I tell him . . . Because he's scaring me. He says I have to tell him about what happened between us if he's going to be able to help me. I tell him he wouldn't understand. He says he's a psycholo . . . psychiatrist . . .

IRENE. Psychologist.

WILLY. Psychologist. It's his job to understand. See what I mean about talking like I'm a child? It's his job to understand. In his . . . In his fake newsreader voice. I says not this. You won't understand this. I'll tell you whatever you want to know, but not this. He says I have to tell him what happened between us. I can't tell him, Irene. There are some things . . . What's important at the moment, he tells me, is that we . . . we determine your mental state and try to make you better. Now, that's a contradiction. Why try to make me better if he doesn't know whether anything's wrong with me or not yet? Which there isn't.

IRENE. I know there isn't.

WILLY. Don't worry about that. Well, I'm sorry doctor, but this bloke's a threat that exists. Don't worry about that. You're not helping, by the way.

IRENE. I . . . What?

WILLY. You're agreeing with me . . .

IRENE. Because you're right.

WILLY. . . . you're . . . And saying nice things, no, not because I'm right. Comforting. Thanks and all, but you're not helping. Comforting words aren't going to help. Action will help. That's all'll do anything for me. A plan of action.

IRENE. But there's nothing you can do at the moment.

WILLY. Except smile.

IRENE. Yeah. Smile and tell the truth.

He laughs to himself. Pause.

Maybe it was the wrong thing.

WILLY. What do you mean?

IRENE. The work you're doing. I always thought you were right for what you *were* doing. When you were in uniform. Talking, you know, to people, communicating and helping people. You're more . . .

WILLY. I'm what?

IRENE. When you're here with me. Or even . . . You're more . . . gentle.

WILLY. Gentle?

IRENE. Or . . . Yeah. Or . . . You communicate well. You know, since . . . . I'd been thinking. You're nice to people.

I didn't think it was right in the first place, you on that
squad. The DS. It's not you, you know? It's aggressive. It's
not the kind of job that your character would suit. (*Pause.
He gives her a dirty look.*)

WILLY. I don't know what you're saying.

IRENE. I'm saying . . .

WILLY. You're saying I'm not cut out for it?

IRENE. No, I'm just . . .

WILLY. Well, now, thanks for that bit of loyalty there, love.
You're saying I'm not man enough for the job. One minute,
you're calling me hardshaw, the next . . .

IRENE. Ah, now, Willy, now.

WILLY. No, now, Irene. You think the other lads are cut out for
it, but poor Willy can't hack it. How can you . . .? How can
you tell, anyway?

IRENE. Willy, don't be silly, now. I'm not saying anything . . .

WILLY. Casting aspersions on my manhood, thank you very
much. My own wife. I made a mistake. I'm not chicken.
I'm not a fucking wimp. I made a mistake.

IRENE. I know.

WILLY. How do you know if I'm man enough for the job or
not?

IRENE. Your character I'm talking about. Your character.

WILLY. I'm of a . . . Less than manly character, that it?

IRENE. I don't know why I'm . . .

The telephone rings. IRENE *answers it.*

Hello? (*Long pause.*) I'd . . . All right. (*To* WILLY.) It's
him.

WILLY *takes the phone.*

WILLY. Hello? (*Pause.*) I'm fine. (*Pause.*) Can you not . . .? I
have a family. (*Pause.*) I'm trying to take care of my family.

(*Pause.*) Can you not . . .? I may lose my job. My wife . . .
(*Long pause. Hangs up.*) The fucking bastard!

IRENE. Willy!

WILLY. The fucker! Do you know what he just said to me?
The f . . .

IRENE. Calm down. This is stupid.

WILLY (*raging*). The . . . Do you . . . Ffff . . .

IRENE. Come on!

WILLY. He . . . Fuck her and fuck you. That's . . . The . . .
He's talking about you! He's . . . The ffffffbollox!

IRENE. Calm down, Willy.

WILLY. Fuck you, he said. To *you.* He said fuck *you.* I'll . . . If
I could . . . I should've done worse. I swear to Christ, I
should've done worse. If I could go back . . .

IRENE. Don't say that, Willy.

WILLY. Fuck him! Making . . . Making phone calls to our
house? Insulting you? My . . . My wife in my own house. If
I could go back, I'm telling you . . .

IRENE. Sit dow . . .

WILLY. The . . .

IRENE. Will you sit down? Sit down. Here.

WILLY. The ffffcccc . . .

*He sits down. She goes to the cabinet and takes out a bottle
of whisky and a glass. She pours the whisky and brings it
over to him.*

Drink that. One go. (*He does. She pours another.*) Go again.
(*He takes it off her. Sips it.*) Now. You're going to . . . Are
you listening? You're going to calm down and think
rationally. These things that are happening to us are . . . Are
you listening to me?

WILLY. Mmm.

IRENE. Look at me, then. These things that are happening to
us are bad. Yes. But what we're going to do is use our heads
and not, do you hear me? Not lose our heads. Not let
ourselves get worked up. We cannot let trials like this get to
us. We've had fairly bad times before and we got through
them, didn't we? We may not get through this easily. We
may have a few losses. The job, or some money . . . I don't
know. If you told me what the hell he was planning. (*He
gives her a look.*) No, but we'll do it like . . . what you were
talking about. Adults. Like civilized human beings. Willy.
(*Pause.*)

WILLY. I just . . . I . . . When I saw him coming towards me, I
. . .

IRENE. I know.

WILLY. I reacted. In a situation like that one, like the one I
was in, you see, I'm telling you, you see someone racing
towards you, you can't just . . .

IRENE. I know.

WILLY. I was caught off guard, but what they don't seem to
understand is that I reacted the way I was taught. The way I
was supposed to. They send me to a bloody psychi . . .

IRENE. Psychologist.

WILLY. To a bloody psychologist? Any one of the others
would have done the same thing. (*Pause.*) You know?
(*Pause.*)

IRENE. Tell me what he's going to write about you.

WILLY. I can't.

IRENE. Of course you can.

WILLY. I can't. It's not . . . It's not me being . . . I physically . . .
I actually physically can't tell you. (*Pause.*) Can you
understand? (*Pause.*) Any of the other lads would've done
the same thing.

IRENE. Bad luck is all it was.

WILLY. I'm not incompetent.

IRENE. I know.

WILLY. I did the right thing.

IRENE. I know you did.

WILLY. I'm trying my best to take care of you.

IRENE. I know you are.

WILLY. But I'm failing.

IRENE. No you're not.

WILLY. But I am.

IRENE. You're not. Willy. You're not. We'll be okay.

WILLY. It's him that needs the psychologist, not me.

IRENE. We'll be okay, Willy.

WILLY. Christ! When I think about what he just did.

IRENE. So what?

WILLY. And what he just said about you.

IRENE. They're only words, Willy. (*Pause.*)

WILLY. Yeah.

IRENE (*silence. WILLY takes a drink*). Is that really true, what you said?

WILLY. What?

IRENE. That they, those people, up in the mountains?

WILLY. What?

IRENE. To keep warm.

WILLY. The Canadians?

IRENE. They smear . . . all over. Is that true?

WILLY. Their shite. Yeah.

IRENE. They don't wear clothes.

WILLY. No. They smear themselves in their own shite. Saw it in the Echo, some professor.

IRENE. God!

WILLY. Professor of Canadian mountain tribes or something.

IRENE. Ah, Willy!

WILLY. Something like that. Had a column, there last week.

IRENE. I couldn't do that.

WILLY. Smear shite?

IRENE. Yeah.

WILLY. If it was cold enough, Irene, you'd smear yourself in anything.

IRENE. The stink.

WILLY. They'd probably like the stink. Wouldn't be a stink to them.

IRENE. Mmm.

WILLY. Soap, now.

IRENE. Soap?

WILLY. Soap, you see. Something like soap, or something we'd see as clean . . .

IRENE. Ah, yeah.

WILLY. Yeah? They'd probably gag if they smelt it. This is what your man was saying. Differences in cultures. (*Pause.*) What's the story on tonight? What are we doing?

IRENE. I don't know. We could go for a drink.

WILLY. Yeah.

IRENE. Or we could stay in.

WILLY. Couple of pints'd be nice. Chat . . . Have a bit of a chat.

IRENE. Yeah.

WILLY. About . . . Not about . . .

IRENE. No.

WILLY. . . . about normal, everyday things.

IRENE. That'd be nice. About . . . We could finish our . . .

WILLY. The Canadians, yeah.

IRENE. You could tell me a bit more.

WILLY. That'd be good.

IRENE. That's interesting.

WILLY. Was an interesting article. Yeah. Want to try and forget about this fucker for a while. (*Pause.*) Well, will we go out, then?

IRENE. Yeah. Do you want to?

WILLY. Yeah, if . . . We'll go out.

IRENE. Yeah. (*Pause.*)

WILLY. I like you.

IRENE. Really? I like you. (*Beat.*) Hardshaw.

WILLY. Couple of pints. (*Pause.*)

IRENE. What time is it? I'll run up and have a quick shower. Will you give Sandra a ring and ask her to come over? Tell her he's already asleep.

WILLY. Right. Hurry up.

IRENE. And, we're desperate.

WILLY. Right.

IRENE *exits.* WILLY *goes to the phone, takes a piece of paper from his pocket and dials a number. He waits.*

Hello. Paul Bolger, please. (*Pause.*) That's strange. (*Pause.*) Hmm. Are you sure? You're sure. All right. Have you any idea where he is? (*Pause.*) All right. That's . . . No, that's fine. I'll call over later. (*Pause.*) No, I'm a friend of his, I'll call over later. I'll be over anyway.

He hangs up. Picks up his glass and drains it. Goes over to door. Calls.

Irene!

IRENE (*calling. Off-stage*). What?

WILLY. Nothing.

He takes his coat from the chair and exits. We stay on the empty room.

IRENE (*calling. Off-stage.*) What?

She comes into the room. Looks around.

Willy? (*Pause.*) Willy?

She stands in the centre of the room.

Blackout.

Scene Four

ADELE*'s house. Breakfast room.* THERESA *sits at the table.* LIZ *pours a couple of brandies and sits down.* THERESA *is understandably nervous.*

THERESA. Is . . . Paul's coming home tonight, isn't he?

LIZ. He is. Adele's looking forward to it.

THERESA. Mmm. How's his form? Is he . . .? How's his walking?

LIZ. I don't know. Says he'll probably have to use crutches for a while. But few weeks, he'll be back to normal. See the ship?

THERESA. Yeah.

LIZ. What d'you think?

THERESA. Yeah.

LIZ. Drink. (*She drinks.*) Right. The reason I asked you down . . .

THERESA. Mmmhmm.

LIZ. I didn't want to tell you over the phone, because I thought it'd be better face to face.

THERESA. All right.

LIZ. The reason . . .

THERESA. Yeah?

LIZ. It's too impersonal over the phone. It's something important that . . . To say it . . .

THERESA. You can't?

LIZ. It's better to be in person, face to face, one on one, having another . . . To have a person, because . . . When I tell you, you'll understand.

THERESA (*pause*). Okay.

LIZ. It's . . . Something like this, eye contact is needed, the presence of . . . and to be able to see the other person, physical and all the other.

THERESA. Right.

LIZ. All right?

THERESA. Yeah.

LIZ. Drink. (*She drinks.*)

THERESA. Now. (*Pause.*)

LIZ. This is a bit . . . (*Pause.*) It's like . . . You see? This is the . . . in the first place, the reason I asked you to come down, because being told something like this over the phone . . . Anyway. I was reading the . . . Some . . . No. Nothing. It might be a shock to discover this. It's a shock, I'm sure, to find out that the love you're giving, you know? The love you're giving is one sided and not being recipro- cated and . . . Are you all right? Are you all right? Drink. Have a drink. (*They both drink.*) I was talking about this subject to Adele. I don't want to . . . Not that it's any of my business. I don't want to see you made a fool of. You're living a lie and I think it's about time you found out about it. (*Pause.*) He's incapable of love.

Silence.

Some . . . It's true. Instinct. That's all it is. By his nature, he
has the incapacity to love. It's . . . It's in his genes, it's all
instinct. Are you okay? I've been through it myself. I don't
know. I'm just saying forget about love because it's an
impossibility. (*Pause.*)

THERESA (*thinking she's been rumbled*). How did you know?

LIZ. Know what?

THERESA. Know about us? How come you knew?

LIZ. I can smell him off you. Sometimes you've got hairs on
you. What do you mean?

THERESA (*confused*). Hairs?

LIZ. His hairs.

THERESA. I . . . (*Pause.*)

LIZ. It's all right. C'mere. Do you want a hug? Come over
here.

THERESA. No, I'm all right.

LIZ. You don't look all right. Sometimes a hug . . .

THERESA. No. No. The . . . (*Pause.*) You can smell him off
me?

LIZ. Not bad. It's nothing you have to be embarrassed about.
(*Pause.*)

THERESA. I feel like a gobshite.

LIZ. Theresa, you didn't know. It's all right. Sure, I only found
out tonight.

THERESA. Does Adele know?

LIZ. Yeah.

THERESA. Oh, Jesus!

LIZ. I told her when I saw it, she was here with me. Don't
worry, you're not a gobshite. She doesn't think so either.

THERESA (*pause*). What did you see?

LIZ. In the paper.

THERESA. The paper?

LIZ. Some professor or other.

THERESA. How does he know?

LIZ. He knows because he's a professor. C'mere. Do you want a hug?

THERESA. No. What do you mean, he knows because he's a professor?

LIZ. He kn . . . 'Cos he's . . . He studies animals. A . . . Behaviour. He's a, a professor of animal behaviour or some such.

THERESA. How does he know about me?

LIZ. He . . . He doesn't know about you. Your dog. Your dog, he knows about.

THERESA. My dog?

LIZ (*pause*). Yeah.

THERESA. Oh! (*Pause.*) My dog.

LIZ. I'm sorry, Theresa. To have to . . . be the one to tell you.

THERESA. My dog doesn't love me is what you're . . .

LIZ. Sometimes if we . . . I'm here for you. If you want a hug, to talk about it, if you want to cry . . .

THERESA. Toby.

LIZ (*pause*). Toby doesn't love you. (*Pause. Drinks.*) Who the hell did you think I was talking about?

THERESA. No, I kne . . .

LIZ. Did . . .?

THERESA. Toby. I knew. Toby.

LIZ. You thought I was talking about something else?

THERESA. No, I knew you were talking about Toby. Sure the, the hairs he leaves on me, etcetera.

LIZ. Yeah!

THERESA. He's an awful shedder. (*Pause.*)

LIZ. How do you feel?

THERESA. I feel all right. I don't know. I didn't know.

LIZ. No, well like I said. I only found out tonight, myself. It's a horrible thing to discover.

THERESA. Hmm.

LIZ. Horrible. But, what? Would you rather have known or not have known?

THERESA (*pause*). Known.

LIZ. That's the way I'd feel. That's the way I'd feel. You don't want to go around living a lie.

Silence.

Who did you think I was talking about?

THERESA. No one. I . . . Toby. I knew.

LIZ. No, you didn't.

THERESA. I did.

LIZ. Do you have a secret?

THERESA. No.

LIZ. Do you have a . . .

THERESA. Stop, would you?

LIZ. . . . . No?

THERESA. I wish I . . .

LIZ. You sure?

THERESA. I wish I did. (*Pause. LIZ drinks.*)

LIZ. So do I. What do you think of the ship?

THERESA. Very nice.

LIZ. Paul's coming home present. (*Calls.*) Adele! (*To* THERESA.) It's a very difficult one.

THERESA. Sure, I'm sure Paul'll be able to handle it.

LIZ. Should pass the time for weeks. The H.M.S Victory.

THERESA. It's big, isn't it.

LIZ (*calling*). Adele! (*She goes to doorway.*) Adele!

ADELE (*off-stage*). Yeah?

LIZ. I was just showing Theresa the . . . Oh, very nice!

ADELE (*off-stage*). Yeah?

THERESA. Adele!

ADELE (*off-stage*). Stop.

LIZ. No. God . . .

THERESA. That's gorgeous.

LIZ. . . . look at you.

THERESA. Adele Bolger!

LIZ. The word glamour is about to be redefined. Come here.

THERESA. Come in.

She enters wearing a sexy white top and black trousers.

LIZ. Give us a twirl. (*She does so.*)

THERESA. Beautiful.

LIZ. Absolutely.

ADELE. Are you sure?

LIZ. Will you . . .? 'Are you sure?' Get out of it.

THERESA. Adele, it's gorgeous.

ADELE. This'll be the first time . . .

LIZ. First time you've worn that combination.

ADELE. Yeah.

THERESA. Lovely.

ADELE. I've worn both of them before, but separately.

THERESA. Right.

ADELE. In different combinations.

LIZ. He'll love it. (*Beat.*)

ADELE (*cheerfully*). I think I'll . . . (*Points at glasses.*)

LIZ. Yeah, yeah. Sit down. I'll get the glass, you vixen.

ADELE. Ah, stop. (*She sits on the couch.* LIZ *gets a glass
  from the press.*)

LIZ. Here we go. You staying, Theresa?

ADELE. I'll . . .

LIZ. Gimme your glass. (*Pours.*) The more the merrier, am I
  right, Adele?

ADELE. Yes.

THERESA. I think I might just . . .

LIZ (*filling her own*). The more. The merrier. (*To* THERESA.)
  How do you feel now? (*To* ADELE.) I told her.

ADELE. Oh. How do you feel?

  ADELE *begins lighting a cigarette. she offers one to*
  THERESA.

THERESA. I'm fine. I'm . . . (*Shakes head at cigarette.*)

LIZ. If you wanna talk about it . . .

THERESA. No. It's not that bad.

  They move to the couch.

LIZ. I just thought you should know.

THERESA. No, I appreciate it.

LIZ. Good.

ADELE. Cheers!

LIZ. Cheers!

THERESA. Cheers! (*They drink.*)

LIZ. So. Any news?

THERESA. I was . . .

LIZ (*interrupting. To* ADELE). What time is it?

ADELE. Twenty to.

THERESA. I . . . think I should be . . .

LIZ. Any scandal, Theresa?

> LIZ *takes the model ship off the table and puts it against the wall to make more room. The girls go into chat mode.* LIZ *returns to her seat.*

THERESA. I was broken into last night.

ADELE. Ah, no.

LIZ. No way. What did they get?

THERESA. Yeah. Telly and the video.

LIZ. Ah, God.

THERESA. Yeah.

LIZ. The bastards.

ADELE. Were you upset?

THERESA. Well, I'm a bit scared since.

ADELE. Living on your own.

THERESA. This is it.

LIZ. Did your dog not bark or . . .?

THERESA. No.

LIZ. Didn't . . .

THERESA. They came in the front.

ADELE. Jesus. Must be . . .

THERESA. It's sort of freaky. Like, since. Say at night time . . .

LIZ. . . . Uhhuh. Yep . . .

THERESA. . . . on my own . . .

LIZ. . . . Must be terrible.

THERESA. Yeah.

LIZ. What do you think of Paul and his injury?

THERESA. It was terrible, wasn't it.

LIZ. It was, all right. He'll come hobbling in, now. See all of us waiting, one two three, bottle of brandy, his new model ship, Adele's sexy attire . . .

ADELE. Ah, Liz.

LIZ. Stop. You know you look great.

ADELE. I look all right.

THERESA. You look great.

LIZ. You look great. (*Pause.*)

THERESA. To think that they were downstairs.

ADELE. Mmm. (*She's a little distressed. Pause.*)

THERESA. It's frightening to think that, while you're asleep, anyone can come in and wander around your house. Your things. Personal . . . I was trying to think of the word. Someone in my house, it made me feel . . . (*Pause.*)

ADELE. You should get an alarm.

LIZ (*with bottle*). Filler upper, Theresa?

THERESA. Eh . . . Well, I don't really know if I should be . . .

LIZ *begins filling the glasses anyway, starting with* THERESA*'s.*

LIZ. Gets you a bit looser, warms up the blood, gives you a nice buzz.

ADELE. Makes it easier to talk.

LIZ. Loose lips sink ships, but what the hell?

Pause. THERESA *picks up her glass.*

THERESA. What the hell? Cheers!

LIZ. Cheers!

ADELE. Cheers! (*They drink.*)

THERESA. Should I get an alarm?

LIZ. An alarm.

ADELE. We have one.

THERESA. I suppose . . .

ADELE. Make you feel safer.

THERESA. That invasion of privacy . . .

ADELE. Paul got one installed in March, we never had a
    problem. The box . . . You can see . . . You know, you can
    see it as you come in. Over the door. I'd say that's a . . .

LIZ. A deterrent.

ADELE. A . . . Yeah. Was reading in the Echo.

LIZ. Sure it is. As much as anything else.

ADELE. A deterrent. Just the sight of it. This professor, what
    was it?

LIZ. 'Cos, yeah. 'Cos they see it.

THERESA. Right.

ADELE. A professor of Burglary Prevention, it was.

THERESA. I'm gonna pop down tomorrow, see if I can get
    one.

ADELE (*to herself*). Home protection?

LIZ. Soon as you can, Theresa.

THERESA. Yeah. (*Pause. They drink.*) Can I use your loo?

LIZ. Sure.

ADELE. Of course.

THERESA. My bladder's just . . .

LIZ. Don't be embarrassed. We're all the same.

ADELE. Go ahead.

THERESA. Thanks.

LIZ. And don't forget to flush. (*She goes. To* ADELE.) Did you get it?

ADELE. What?

LIZ. Did you smell it?

ADELE. No.

LIZ. Yes, you did.

ADELE. Liz, that's not nice.

LIZ. I'm just asking you.

ADELE. That's not nice. (*Pause.*)

LIZ. But, did you smell it?

ADELE. Yes.

LIZ. I told you.

ADELE. Right. Enough.

LIZ. I told you you could smell it.

ADELE. Right. (*Pause.*)

LIZ. Did you see the hairs?

ADELE. What? Liz! No.

LIZ. They're on her jumper. She a . . .

ADELE. I di . . .

LIZ. . . . She always has them.

ADELE. No.

LIZ. You didn't?

ADELE. No, I didn't. You're mean.

LIZ. Just observant, Adele. You'll see when she comes down.

ADELE. Right.

LIZ. Have a look.

ADELE. Right. (*Beat.*) No! (*Pause. Then in shocked tone.*) No! (*Pause.*) How'd she take the news?

LIZ. Ssshhh! (THERESA *enters.*) Did you flush?

THERESA. Of course I did. I always flush.

LIZ. I'm joking. Sit down. (*She sits.*) I'm joking. (*To* ADELE.) Is this the last bottle? (ADELE *shakes her head.*) Stupid question. (*They laugh. Pause.* THERESA *leans confidentially towards* ADELE.)

THERESA. How are you feeling these days, Adele?

Obviously she's said the wrong thing. LIZ *comes to the rescue, interrupting* THERESA.

LIZ. You should get that alarm. Now that it's happened, they might think you're easy pickings. They might come back. Might come upstairs next time.

THERESA (*alarmed*). Yeah?

LIZ. Get that alarm. Security is the best policy.

ADELE. It is.

LIZ. 'Less you *want* them to . . .

THERESA. What?

LIZ. That right, Adele?

ADELE. Which?

LIZ. Up the old bedroom.

THERESA. Ah, no. No.

ADELE. Liz!

LIZ. Up the old bedroom. What?!!

THERESA. No way.

LIZ. A good ravaging, now?

ADELE. Liz!

THERESA. You wouldn't!

LIZ. All depends, now, Theresa. All depends. I don't know.

They are interrupted by the sound of a key in the door. Enter PAUL. *He hobbles in slowly on his walking stick.*

PAUL. How's it going?

ADELE. Heya, Paul.

LIZ. Heya, Paul.

THERESA. Hello, Paul.

PAUL. Heya, Theresa.

He makes to take off his jacket.

LIZ. Hold it. Wait. Paul. Let me do that. (*She does.*)

PAUL. Thanks.

LIZ (*helping him sit down*). Down. Now. All right?

PAUL. Yep. Thanks.

LIZ. No problem at all. Do you want some brandy?

PAUL. Yeah. Nice one. Dropped in for a pint on my merry way already. (LIZ *goes to get a glass.*) How are things?

ADELE. Fine. How's your hip?

PAUL (*dismissively*). Agh!

ADELE. Does it hurt much?

PAUL. No, sometimes. Not much. Something strange going on here.

LIZ sits back down with glass and begins to pour for PAUL.

ADELE. What?

LIZ. Something strange, Paul?

PAUL. Mmm.

LIZ. Do you notice something, Theresa?

THERESA. Me?

LIZ. Yeah.

THERESA. No.

PAUL. Adele?

ADELE. What?

PAUL. Do you notice something strange?

ADELE. I . . . I don't know. (*Pause.*)

PAUL. Hmm. (*Pause. He looks* ADELE *up and down.*)

LIZ. Ah, Paul!

PAUL (*still looking at* ADELE). What?

LIZ. Stop it.

THERESA. What?

ADELE. I . . .

PAUL. Sexy as hell. (ADELE *laughs.*)

LIZ. Paul.

PAUL. Look at you.

ADELE. Well, you . . .

PAUL. Look at the sexy lady.

LIZ. Isn't she?

PAUL. Look at you.

ADELE. You were coming home. (*Beat.*)

PAUL. For me?

LIZ. Yeah.

PAUL. Yeah?

ADELE. I thought . . .

PAUL. No. No . . .

ADELE. . . . I thought . . .

PAUL. You thought right, Adele. No. You thought right. (*To* LIZ.) I see you didn't make any effort.

LIZ. Go to hell.

PAUL (*to* ADELE). Stand up. (*She stands.*) That's beautiful.

ADELE. The combination.

PAUL. That's what it is. Can I have a kiss? (*She kisses him, then sits down.*) This is nice. (*He drinks.*) How are things, Theresa?

THERESA. Fine.

PAUL. Long time no see.

THERESA. Yeah.

LIZ. Theresa was broken into the other night.

PAUL. Yeah?

LIZ. Robbed her telly and her video.

PAUL (*to* THERESA). Yeah?

THERESA. Just my telly and my video.

PAUL. You were lucky. (*To* ADELE.) Look at you.

ADELE. Stop.

LIZ. I told her she should get an alarm.

PAUL. You should. You should.

THERESA. I'm going to have a look tomorrow.

PAUL. You should. (*He drinks.*) Agh! (*Pause.*)

ADELE. Are you glad to be out?

PAUL. Too right. The nurses in there.

THERESA. Nice?

PAUL. Rough. You must be joking. Big . . . Awfully rough they
are. Picking you up and putting you down. Big matrons
treating me like a sack of potatoes. (*To* ADELE.) I was
telling you.

LIZ. You poor thing.

PAUL (*to* ADELE). You'll be gentle with me, won't you.
'Course you will. I need a gentle hand at the moment. You
look gorgeous.

ADELE. Thanks.

PAUL. My special pal.

ADELE. *My* special pal.

THERESA *almost does a double take at this.*

LIZ. Adele. (*Makes a signalling motion with her head.* ADELE
gets the model ship.)

PAUL. What's . . . For me?

ADELE. Yeah.

PAUL (*taking it*). Oh, brilliant.

ADELE (*sitting down*). That's to pass the time.

PAUL. Brilliant.

ADELE. Liz picked it out.

LIZ. I did not. (PAUL *is opening the box.*)

ADELE. You did so.

LIZ. Well, you paid for it.

ADELE. *We* paid for it.

PAUL (*taking out pieces and looking at them*). Well, thanks the
pair of you. What do you think, Theresa?

THERESA. It's lovely.

PAUL. Look at the size of those pieces.

LIZ. What's that? A gun?

PAUL. A cannon. Jesus. That'll take a while.

ADELE. Well, it's to pass the time. (*Pause.*)

PAUL. Thank you. (*Kisses her.*) Thanks.

THERESA. Maybe I should get something like that, now that I've no telly.

PAUL *has broken the little cannon off its frame. He shoots* THERESA *with it, making the sound with his mouth.*

PAUL. Size of them.

LIZ. It's got every little detail.

THERESA. Have you ever done one of those before, Paul?

PAUL. Not . . . When I was a little boy, I used to. But not in years.

ADELE. Who were you in the pub with?

PAUL. On my lonesome.

LIZ. There's no stopping him, he's only out of the hospital.

ADELE. Why were you on your own?

PAUL. Ah, I just had to have a think about things. It's a big deal getting out and coming home. Make a few plans, I wanted to get my head together a bit. Just to. . . 'Cos whether I like it or not, life's gonna be a bit different from now on. Things changed the minute that fu . . . Soon as it happened. Isn't it amazing? Little event like that. An occurrence . . . Still . . . (*To* ADELE.) We can talk about stuff later if you want.

ADELE. Yeah. If you want. (PAUL *takes a drink.*)

PAUL. So, how come you're here, Theresa?

THERESA. We . . .

LIZ. Paul!

PAUL. I'm only asking. I'm not being rude. (*To* THERESA.) Was I being rude?

THERESA. No.

PAUL. I wasn't. I was just asking. I didn't expect.

LIZ. I asked her down.

PAUL. You rang her, did you?

LIZ. Yeah.

PAUL. Right.

THERESA. Liz read something in the paper and she felt she
should . . .

LIZ. About dogs, Paul. Do you know that dogs are incapable
of love?

PAUL. What?

LIZ. This professor in tonight's paper says so.

PAUL (*kissing* ADELE). Thanks for the model.

ADELE. You're welcome.

LIZ. Dogs, Paul. It's not in their gene structure to be capable
of love.

PAUL. Dogs.

LIZ. Here, it's . . . (*She hands him the newspaper.*) There.

PAUL (*taking a quick glance*). That's rubbish.

LIZ. He says so.

PAUL. Doesn't make it true. What do you think, Theresa?

THERESA. Yeah, I . . .

PAUL. Doesn't make it true.

LIZ. Well, that's why . . . I wanted to tell Theresa. (*Pause.*)

PAUL (*to* THERESA). That your dog doesn't love you.

THERESA. Yeah.

PAUL (*to* LIZ). You're fucked.

LIZ. It says so there, Paul.

PAUL (*to* THERESA). She got you all the way down here.
(*Pause. Reads.*) A professor of canine psychology. That

should tell you. The only bloke worth reading in that rag is
Tony Kelly. Do you ever read him, Theresa? Crime
correspondent?

THERESA. Em . . . I don't . . .

PAUL. Good bloody writer.

THERESA. Is he?

PAUL. Genius, he is. Very good.

ADELE. I have to go to the weewee. (*She rises and exits.*)

LIZ. Don't forget to flush.

PAUL. Look at her strut.

LIZ (*to* THERESA). I'm only messing. (*To herself.*) Where's
the . . .? (*Calling.*) Where's the other bottle, Adele?

ADELE (*off-stage*). What?

LIZ. The other bottle.

ADELE (*off-stage*). What about it?

LIZ. Where is it?

ADELE (*off-stage*). It's in the cabinet inside.

LIZ. Right. (*To others.*) You on for some more?

PAUL. Pour away. (*She pours.*)

LIZ. The more, the merrier, huh?

PAUL. Yep.

THERESA. That's enough. Thanks.

LIZ. I'll just get another one.

LIZ *exits. While she is gone,* PAUL *and* THERESA *look
very uncomfortable. Each looks down at the table as if the
other isn't there.* LIZ *returns with another bottle of brandy
and sits down.*

PAUL (*drinks. Confidentially to* LIZ). How is she?

LIZ. She's fine.

PAUL. Everything's . . .

LIZ. Yeah. She's grand.

PAUL. Who bought the ship?

LIZ (*beat*). I did. (*Beat.*) She's grand. (*Pause.*)

PAUL. This fucking adventure's all she needs.

THERESA. Will I head on?

PAUL. No.

LIZ. No. No. Theresa.

PAUL. Sure, you're here.

LIZ. Have a drink. You've started. (*They drink.*)

PAUL. What do you think of this dog business, Theresa?

THERESA. The . . . What Liz said?

PAUL. Yeah.

THERESA. I don't know. It wouldn't really effect me much. If
    . . . I mean, it's true. Then that's . . . I don't know if it'd
    make any difference to me. I like my dog.

PAUL. Do you belie . . .?

THERESA. It's not a person, though. It's only a dog.

LIZ. But you like it.

THERESA. Yeah.

LIZ. You like it a lot.

THERESA. It's a dog. I like it as . . .

PAUL. But do you believe about . . .?

THERESA. I like it . . .

LIZ. A lot.

PAUL. But do you believe what Liz said?

LIZ. I didn't say it, I . . .

PAUL. Well in the paper.

LIZ. The professor.

PAUL. Do you?

THERESA. Do . . . I don't know. But, even if it's true . . .

PAUL. It's not.

LIZ. It could be.

THERESA. It wouldn't effect me, I don't think. It's only a
dog, so I don't really mind. Lovewise. Long as it's there,
especially now after the . . . the burglary, I'm glad there's
somebody around. What's the word I'm trying to think of?
Anyway, love me or not, he can still provide me with some
company.

Enter ADELE *looking upset again.*

PAUL. Okay?

ADELE (*sitting down*). Yeah. (*He kisses her.*)

PAUL. Do you believe it?

ADELE (*distant*). What?

PAUL. About the dog. Are you all right?

ADELE (*upset*). I'm . . . Yeah. Just a . . . Gimme . . .

LIZ. Adele?

ADELE. I'm a bit . . .

PAUL. D'you need . . .?

ADELE. There's . . . Gimme two minutes.

LIZ. You all right, Adele?

ADELE. Gimme . . . Yeah. Leave . . . (*Pause. Upset. To*
PAUL.) Someone rang.

LIZ. Oh, that's right!

PAUL (*to* ADELE). Who rang?

ADELE (*starting to cry*). Someone.

    ADELE *gets up and leaves the room, distressed.* PAUL *gets
    up and follows.*

PAUL. Adele!

THERESA. Should I go?

LIZ. No, no, she's all right. (*Calling.*) She all right, Paul?

PAUL (*off-stage. Calling*). Yeah, she's grand.

THERESA. I think I should go. I shouldn't really . . .

LIZ. Stay where you are. She . . . It'll pass in a minute. (*Very serious.*) Theresa. Adele's a bit ill.

THERESA. Well, should I not go, then?

LIZ. No, no, no, you're grand. She sometimes gets a bit confused or addled or frustrated, something. She's all right. Paul knows. Bit sick. Kind of a nervous . . . Stressful situations, you know? She has these fits. Falls down, so she needs to be, you know. Nothing major, now, it doesn't damage her or anything, but they take a while to pass. Kinda . . . (*Demonstrates a fit.*) you know? But not dangerous.

THERESA. I . . .

LIZ. She's fine, she's pills, she's not having one now. Stay put, we're having a few drinks.

There is a knock on the door.

Who's this, now?

LIZ *goes out to answer it.*

We hear the door opening.

(*off-stage.*) Yes?

VOICE (*off-stage*). Is eh . . . Paul Bolger home, please?

LIZ (*off-stage*). Yyeees. Who shall I say it is?

VOICE (*off-stage*). I'm the man who shot him.

Blackout.

ACT TWO

Scene One

The same. A few minutes later. PAUL *sits on the sofa.* WILLY *stands. They are alone.*

PAUL *and* WILLY.

WILLY. You were running. You were running, you were coming towards me.

PAUL. Trying to stay out of trouble.

WILLY. But, yeah, but when it happened, all I could think about was . . .

PAUL. How powerful you were.

WILLY. No. What?

PAUL. We talked about this at the hospital. Think you've got the power and the right.

WILLY. Right to what?

PAUL. Right to do things.

WILLY. Do what?

PAUL. Do stuff and all, going around shooting guns.

WILLY. Shooting?

PAUL. Shooting guns and all, going around in your cars, flying around, skidding. I know youse.

WILLY. I'd never shot my gun before, shot it at a person.

PAUL. Going around, then.

WILLY. What?

PAUL. Going around in your cars, flying around.

WILLY. Well . . .

PAUL. Deny that, you fucker.

WILLY. . . . sometimes we . . .

PAUL. Ah-ha. Think youse are it. Can you deny it?

WILLY. . . . Sometimes we drive fast.

PAUL. Right.

WILLY. But we don't think we're it. 'Least I don't.

PAUL. 'Cos you're not.

WILLY. What?

PAUL. You're not it.

WILLY. I don't think I am.

PAUL. Think you're Don Johnson or something?

WILLY. It wasn't my fault.

PAUL. Whose fault was it?

WILLY. It was an accident.

PAUL. Well, maybe if you'd've been a bit more careful, now. Don Johnson doesn't shoot without thinking.

WILLY. It was . . .

PAUL. Don Johnson takes aim.

WILLY. Too much was going on. I didn't have time to think.

PAUL. You'd more time than me. I didn't have any time.

WILLY. I know.

PAUL. Time enough to feel pain.

WILLY. I'm sorry.

PAUL. On my merry way 'round the corner, BANG! Time enough to go into shock, know what I'm saying? On my merry way home to my wife. You could've killed me. You could've easily hit me somewhere else.

WILLY. I know, I . . .

PAUL. In the head or something, got me. In the heart. Could've blown my head off, Jaysus! In my eye or something.

WILLY. If I . . .

PAUL. Jaysus!

WILLY. If I could . . .

PAUL. In my . . . Shut up, will you? Shut your mouth. You're in my house, have the common decency not to start interrupting me. As soon as . . .

WILLY. I'm sorry, I . . .

PAUL. . . . Will you? You're doing it again.

WILLY. I'm sorry.

PAUL. This isn't some gangster's . . . hideout you're doing a . . . thing on, this is my house. (*Pause.*) What was I . . .? My belly. Shot in the belly can kill you. Shot in the chest, doesn't even have to be your heart. Where else? The eye, now'd be the worst. See what I'm saying? See how serious what you did is?

WILLY. I know how serious it is.

PAUL. What d'you want?

WILLY. I came for . . . To ask you . . .

PAUL. Ask me what?

WILLY. To stop.

PAUL. Never.

WILLY. Please.

PAUL. I will never, I will never.

WILLY. But . . .

PAUL. I will never.

WILLY. Tell me why, then.

PAUL. You know why. Look at the state of me. I'm in flitters. My hip's in flits, I can't walk without my stick. In tatters,

I am. See that? That's all I'll be doing for the next few weeks, now, 'cos of you. Sitting on my arse, trying to build the, whatsit?

WILLY. H.M.S Victory.

PAUL. The H.M.S Victory. Recovering. There's a few weeks of my life wasted, now. On that fucking thing.

WILLY. That's a beautiful ship.

PAUL. That's not what I'm on about.

WILLY. I know it's not.

PAUL. I know it's a beautiful ship.

LIZ (*entering from up stairs*). Sorry, Paul.

PAUL. What are you . . .?

LIZ (*indicating brandy bottle*). Can I . . .?

PAUL. Yeah. Go on. Hang on. (*Pours himself a glass.*)

LIZ (*to* WILLY). Nice, isn't it?

WILLY. Lovely.

LIZ. Should keep him occupied for weeks, now.

PAUL. How is she?

LIZ. Ah, she's fine. You know.

PAUL. Good. How's Theresa?

LIZ (*beat*). She's fine, too.

PAUL. Good.

LIZ (*taking bottle*). Jaysus, she's gas, isn't she?

PAUL. Who?

LIZ. Theresa. C'mere. Did you notice . . .? (*Looks at* WILLY.) I'll ask you after. (*Exits.*)

WILLY. Do you have a family?

PAUL. None of your . . . No. I have a wife.

WILLY. Her?

PAUL. You must be joking.

WILLY. Your wife . . .

PAUL. Don't talk about her.

WILLY. My wife.

PAUL. Yours.

WILLY. My son. It's not just me you're hurting. My family had nothing to do with anything. When they read it . . . They're going to be hurt and they did nothing.

PAUL. That's life, man. It's like me being shot, you know? Kind of stuff happens.

WILLY. What the hell were you doing there?

PAUL. I told you before, a mate of mine lives there. The whole block isn't criminal. See, it's this kind of attitude, now . . .

WILLY. I wasn't saying . . .

PAUL. . . . . this attitude, just because someone lives in a place . . .

WILLY. I wasn't . . .

PAUL. You think you can judge these innocent people who don't have the money to live anywhere else?

WILLY. I don't.

PAUL. And this kind of fucking attitude, now. This kind of attitude, going around firing your gun, could take someone's eye out.

WILLY. Yeah.

PAUL. Could you imagine? (*Pause.*)

WILLY. When you phoned my house tonight and what you said to me. To my wife. About my wife.

PAUL. What did I say?

WILLY. You said fuck her. You said fuck me and . . .

PAUL. Fuck you.

WILLY. What did she do to you?

PAUL. Look. I said it. I meant I don't care. I don't know your wife, if she happens to get hurt, then . . . You know.

WILLY. Let me tell you this. Let me tell you this, waiting to go out and get someone, it's not exciting, it's far from exciting. Maybe for the other lads. I'm telling you this, now . . .

PAUL. I'm not particularly interested.

WILLY. Let me tell you this. This is just now, to, if I could make you understand the, the . . . pressures . . . inherent.

PAUL. Go on. Fuck sake!

WILLY. That day, the day it happened was a Friday, we were sitting in the office, I was only on the squad two weeks, we were sitting in the office waiting for a phone call, could get a phone call from any number of snitches . . .

PAUL. Snitches?

WILLY. Yeah.

PAUL. Like in . . .

WILLY. In . . . On telly, yeah. That's what we call them as well.

PAUL. Right.

WILLY. We've warrants there for three or four dealers and we're waiting to see which one we'll get a snitch on. Sitting there filling in the warrants.

PAUL. You fill them in first?

WILLY. Just so we won't have to worry about it later. Still have to get the district judge's signature. So, the phone call comes.

PAUL. Snitch.

WILLY. One of the snitches. This fella, Maurice Joyce.

PAUL. The snitch.

WILLY. No, the fella.

PAUL. Oh, right. Who youse're . . .

WILLY. Who we're, yeah, who we're . . .

PAUL. Uhhuh.

WILLY. Snitch gives us the address and the squad goes mad, 'cos Maurice Joyce's wanted for murder on top of being a dealer. That couple shot up at Whiteoaks. Did you . . .?

PAUL. I did, I read it.

WILLY. Two of them shot in the head.

PAUL. In The Echo. Tony Kelly column.

WILLY. I don't want to go up against a murderer. I don't want to put myself in that situation. I'm telling you this, now. I'm telling you this so maybe you'll . . .

PAUL. Right.

WILLY. So you'll maybe . . .

PAUL. So youse get the info. The tip.

WILLY. The squad goes mad, we're gonna catch a killer, we'll get a curry after to celebrate. Off we go, straight to the detective commisioner's house, he's out in the garden trimming his hedges. We skid up . . .

PAUL. Skid up, yeah? See what I'm saying?

WILLY. I wasn't driving.

PAUL. Strange, though, isn't it? Youse skid up.

WILLY. We're in a hurry to get there, 'case he leaves.

PAUL. Go on.

WILLY. This is my first time, now. Judge signs the warrant, good luck lads, off we go.

PAUL. Pull a handbreaker off, yeah?

WILLY. I don't remember. We go to the flat. Maurice Joyce is the third floor. The lads are still discussing curries.

PAUL. What's this about curries?

WILLY. Whenever they do a successful job, they have a curry.

PAUL. Very good. Pint's not good enough for them, no?

WILLY. It's just a thing they do.

PAUL. More elitist behaviour, you see? Handbreakers, curry, go on. Fuckers thinking they're it, go on.

WILLY. We get out the battering ram.

PAUL. Youse have a battering ram?

WILLY. To knock the door down.

PAUL. Right.

WILLY. Knock on the door . . .

PAUL. What are youse knocking on the door for if youse have a battering ram?

WILLY. Have to knock on the door and identify youself.

PAUL. I'd just plow my way in, surprise them.

WILLY. That's the rules.

PAUL. That's a bit stupid now. Giving them a chance? I'd knock the fucking door down, catch them in the act, don't give them the fucking chance, the bastards.

WILLY. I know.

PAUL. Go on, go on. Youse knock on the door . . .

WILLY. We knock on the door, tell them it's the DS, we've a warrant.

PAUL. DS?

WILLY. Drug Squad.

PAUL. 'Course.

WILLY. Then we knock down the door. Have to do it as quick as possible before they flush the stuff down the jacks or swallow it.

PAUL. Right. After . . .

WILLY. Run inside . . .

PAUL. . . . after giving them a warning.

WILLY. It's the rules.

PAUL. It's stupid. Go on.

WILLY. Get inside and there's no-one there.

PAUL. But your . . .

WILLY. The snitch. I know.

PAUL. He told youse a lie.

WILLY. Well, they could've been there when he said, but . . .

PAUL. Right. Right. In the meantime . . .

WILLY. . . . Time we get the warrant signed and all.

PAUL. Which is why youse fill them out at the station.

WILLY. Save time.

PAUL. Right. That's smart, now.

WILLY. So, in we go.

PAUL. Smart thinking. How many of youse is there?

WILLY. Three men and one woman.

PAUL. You're the woman, yeah?

WILLY. No, I'm not the woman.

PAUL. Does the woman have a gun as well?

WILLY. No. She's there to . . .

PAUL. Good. Go on. This is interesting.

WILLY. I'm telling you this, now, so you'll know what I
    was . . . what I was thinking. My . . .

PAUL. Yeah. Yeah. It's interesting.

WILLY. . . . kind of pressure I was under.

PAUL. Youse get into the flat and there's no-one there.

WILLY. And there's no-one there. Hear someone calling
     outside. Youngfella at the front door about sixteen, strung
     out to fuck, says, 'Is Maurice there?' Door's on the ground
     and he doesn't even notice.

PAUL. No way.

WILLY. Strung out to fuck.

PAUL. Doesn't even notice the door!

WILLY. He just wants a fix, so I tell him Joey's not here. So,
     he's, 'Ah, I'm dying for a fix, man,' giving it all that, and
     then, 'Ah, sure here he is.' Maurice Joyce and four or five
     other blokes come around the corner, the walkway,
     McDonalds bags in their arms. They spot us, we spot them,
     out with the guns, us and them. McDonalds up in the air,
     they scatter, everybody scatters, running downstairs into
     other flats, disappearing, firing their guns behind them.
     Guess what Maurice Joyce shouts?

PAUL. What?

WILLY. Youse'll never take me alive.

PAUL. Jaysus!

WILLY. Thing is, he meant it.

PAUL. Murder rap on him.

WILLY. Exactly. Rest of the squad flies after them and I was
     left standing there like a fool. All happened so fast, I'm left
     thinking, where the fuck did everyone go? Wondering what
     to do and then you come along. Flying around the corner,
     running towards me, running at me.

PAUL. On my merry way home, that's all.

WILLY. I panicked. Do I shoot, do I run?

PAUL. Innocent me on my merry fucking way.

WILLY. All in a split second. Do I fight? Am I gonna die? I
     pointed my gun and . . . I overreacted, I panicked, it was all
     so fast, I pointed my gun and I fired. (*Pause.*) Now.

PAUL (*pause.*) Now what?

WILLY. I told you what happened. I told you how scared I
was. D'you see the, the confusion, the pressure I was
under? I was scared. I've admitted it to you. D'you see what
kind of . . .?

PAUL. Admitted what?

WILLY. I was scared, I was confused, I . . .

PAUL. Admitted what? I'm sitting here . . . I'm sitting here
listening to you telling me how cool the fucking drug squad
is.

WILLY. What?

PAUL. Your guns and your cars, skidding up to the judge's
gaff, with your battering rams, you're boasting. Poor little
junkie, too strung out to notice a broken door and youse use
it as a source of mockery?

WILLY. It's what happened.

PAUL. Tony Kelly's got a way with fucking words, hasn't he.
(*Pause.*)

WILLY. I've given you this. I've told you stuff I wouldn't even
tell my wife.

PAUL. What have you given me?

WILLY. Something . . . I'm trying to . . . Something of myself.

PAUL. Of your . . .

WILLY. Yes, of . . .

PAUL. You didn't tell me everything.

WILLY. What?

PAUL. What happened when you shot me, you know? What's
this all about?

WILLY. Well, you saw that.

PAUL. I'd my mind on the bullets in me.

WILLY. I told you, the pressure . . . The, the . . . I told you
how I was . . .

PAUL. I wasn't really concentrating.

WILLY. The pressure . . . (*Pause.* PAUL *stands up.*)

PAUL. You pissed yourself. The man from the drug squad pissed himself.

WILLY. I don't want people to know.

PAUL. I was lying on the ground with two bullets in me, did I cry? I took what happened like a man. I didn't lose control of my bladder like a woman.

WILLY. Stop.

PAUL. How can you live with yourself, no I won't stop. I have to let people know there's a woman in the drug squad, you sad bastard. Down on your knees, whingeing like a three year old, going weewee like a baby. 'Awww. I'm sorry. I didn't mean it. Awww . . .!' Me down there filled with hot lead, I didn't wet myself. Oh, no. And I saw you tying your jacket around your waist, you sneaky fucker. Least I know how to bite the bullet. Least I can take it. Youse all think you're such fucking men.

WILLY. Stop it. Stop that fucking . . .

PAUL. What'll you do? Cry?

WILLY. Just don't . . .

PAUL. Weewee in your drawers? You baby, you woman. Don Johnson wouldn't've pissed himself no matter who he shot. Don's like me. Don can bite the bullet.

WILLY. Don't print this. Please. My wife . . .

PAUL. Ah, now.

WILLY. I'm being punished. I'm seeing a psychologist.

PAUL. Why?

WILLY. Because . . .

PAUL. Because you go around shooting people?

WILLY. No, because . . .

PAUL. Because you've a bed wetting problem?

WILLY. He tells me I could be suffering from whatsit? Post stress . . . Post shooting something or other. They're trying to see if . . . They're trying to see if I'm incompetent.

PAUL. Incontinent?

WILLY. Incompetent. Do you not understand?

PAUL. Tony Kelly's good at the old word play, isn't he? I wonder how he'll write this up, now. See if he'll make up a bit of word play using them words. Incompetent and . . .

WILLY. What can I do?!!!

PAUL. Listen to me. You're wasting your time.

WILLY. If you could . . .

PAUL. You're wasting your time, Mister incontinent. Read all about it. Think you can come in here, showing off with your drug squad stories, thinking you're Don, with your guns and your cars and your fucking curries, thinking you're Don, thinking you're fucking great.

WILLY. You're . . .

PAUL. Telling me stories? (*Long pause.*)

WILLY. You're jealous, you cunt.

PAUL. What?

WILLY. You're fucking jealous of me?

PAUL. Of piss in the bed? Calling me a cunt in my own gaff?

WILLY. What the fuck have you got to be jealous about?

PAUL. Go and ask my . . .

WILLY. You were well in there. Right up to the end.

PAUL. I was interested.

WILLY. You're jealous. You cunt.

PAUL. Calling me a . . . Calling me a . . . (*Impersonating him.*) 'Awwww!'

WILLY. You're . . . You're . . .

PAUL. 'Awwww!'

WILLY. I don't belie . . .

PAUL. 'Pssss. Pssss. I didn't mean it. Awwww!'

LIZ (*off*). You fucking bastard! (*She enters from upstairs.*)

PAUL. 'Awwww!'

LIZ. I said you bastard.

PAUL. What?

LIZ (*calling up stairs*). Get your fucking arse down here!!

PAUL (*to* WILLY). You've to go. Talk's over. Finished.

LIZ. Theresa!

PAUL (*to* WILLY). Get out! (*To* LIZ.) What's up?

WILLY. If I could . . . Another time . . .

PAUL. What?

WILLY. If I could . . .

PAUL. Read all about it. Tony Kelly. Crime correspondent. The Echo.

LIZ (*calling up stairs*). Theresa! Get your hole down here!

PAUL (*to* WILLY). Now! Out! (WILLY *leaves.*)

LIZ. How dare you? (THERESA *enters from up stairs.*)

THERESA. Em . . . She's em . . .

PAUL. What's going on?

LIZ. Guess, you thick.

THERESA. You're wrong, Liz.

LIZ. I'm . . .

THERESA. You're wrong.

PAUL. What the fuck is . . .?

LIZ. I'm wrong?

PAUL. Making a show of us in front of . . .

LIZ (*to* PAUL). You fuckhead. (*To* THERESA.) You certainly
made a . . . (*To* PAUL.) You fuckhead. All she wanted . . .
(*To* THERESA.) You should've kept you big mouth shut.

THERESA. Liz. This is all . . . There's a . . .

ADELE (*off*). Get her out, get her out!!

PAUL. What happened? What are you . . .? (*Calling.*) Adele!!

THERESA. You're thinking stupid, the wrong things.

LIZ. Don't you . . .

THERESA. How can you . . .?

LIZ. Don't do that.

PAUL (*calling*). Adele!!

LIZ. You're no man, Paul Bolger.

THERESA. What's she talking about?

PAUL. Liz. What are you . . .?

LIZ. You know fucking well. The dark trick. (*To* THERESA.)
The dark fucking trick. Get out.

THERESA. Paul.

PAUL. You'd better head on.

LIZ. Get out.

ADELE (*off*). Get her out!! (*Pause.* THERESA *exits house.*
Pause.)

PAUL. What's going on?

LIZ. What kind of a husband are you?

PAUL. You're in my house, Liz.

LIZ. What kind of a man . . . ? I don't give a good fuck whose
house I'm in. That poor girl up . . . That poor girl . . .

PAUL. Liz.

LIZ. Shame on you, you mouse.

PAUL. What were you drinking?

LIZ. Same as you. Shame on you. She's up there. She's up there. I'm trying to take care . . .

PAUL (*calling*). Adele!! Adele!! (LIZ *goes upstairs.*) Adele!!

    Blackout.

Scene Two

Morning. PAUL *is sitting on the edge of the sofa in his underwear. A blanket thrown off him.* LIZ *is making breakfast throughout scene.*

LIZ. We all feel the same.

PAUL. We don't all feel the same. I should have something flat to sleep on for my hip. I've to keep my back straight. (*Pause.*) Look at the dip in that.

LIZ. You should have slept on the floor, then.

PAUL. Look at that.

LIZ. I see it.

PAUL. I'm not sleeping on the floor. (*Pause.*) My bed's straight, now. Big pit in the middle of it. (*Pause.*) Tough night, Liz.

LIZ. Yeah.

PAUL. Where's my stick?

LIZ. Where'd you leave it?

PAUL. Well, if I knew that . . . Ah, fuck it. What happened, Liz?

LIZ. She opened her big mouth, how could you?

PAUL. I'm only human.

LIZ. Bit of self control, Paul.

PAUL. What happened?

LIZ. We were upstairs talking about Theresa's burglary and she was telling us how scared she was when she's on her own. She was scared about this and she needed someone to listen to her, to understand, and she said . . . Bit of attention, you know? And she said, 'When Paul's there . . .' That's what she said. 'When Paul's there . . .' Then she shut her mouth and you could see she knew she fucked up. Course we copped it.

PAUL. That could mean . . .

LIZ. Copped it goodo.

PAUL. That could mean anything.

LIZ. But it doesn't mean anything, does it?

PAUL. Going through a difficult patch, Liz.

LIZ. So am I.

PAUL. Difficult time in my life.

LIZ. So am I, so's Adele.

PAUL. With this bloke, this copper. I've to see things through.

LIZ. See what through?

PAUL. Ah, now.

LIZ. See what?

PAUL. Ah, now . . . You know?

LIZ. See? D'you see, Paul?

PAUL. What? (*Pause.*) Can I've a . . .?

LIZ. Get it yourself.

She goes upstairs. PAUL *looks for his stick, then goes to his model ship. Sits down at table. Opens box. A knock on the door. He goes out and opens it. His and* IRENE's *voices are heard off-stage.*

IRENE. Hello.

PAUL. Yes?

IRENE. I'm . . . Willy's wife.

PAUL. Who's Willy?

IRENE. Willy's the . . . the man who shot you.

PAUL. Sent you around, did he?

IRENE. No, he didn't. Can I come in?

PAUL. I'm only up.

IRENE. Just for a minute.

PAUL. I don't know. Wife of the enemy. Haven't got my wits about me yet.

IRENE. I won't keep you.

PAUL. Did he send you around?

IRENE. No, he didn't.

PAUL. I'm only up.

IRENE. Just for a . . .

PAUL. Jaysus! (*Pause.*) For a minute.

They enter.

IRENE. I just wondered if you'd seen him.

PAUL. I saw . . .

IRENE. You saw him.

PAUL. I saw . . . Last night.

IRENE. He didn't come home.

PAUL. To your gaff?

IRENE. Yes. No.

PAUL. Oh.

IRENE. He didn't come home, I waited up all night for him, you see, you see, we were going to go for a drink and I went up for a shower and . . .

PAUL. Look at that couch.

IRENE. What?

PAUL. Lie down on that couch.

IRENE. I will not.

PAUL. See how it dips in the middle?

IRENE. I see it.

PAUL. Good.

IRENE. You saw him?

PAUL. He was here last night, causing hassle.

IRENE. How are you?

PAUL. I'm crip . . .

IRENE. Is he here?

PAUL. No.

IRENE. No?

PAUL. He left.

IRENE. How are you?

PAUL. I'm crippled and I'm imp . . .

IRENE (*interrupting*). No. No. I don't care. Did he say where he was going?

PAUL. No. (*Pause.*)

IRENE. What are you going to write about him?

PAUL. You'll see it.

IRENE. Is it bad?

PAUL. I don't know. You mightn't think so.

IRENE. Why not?

PAUL. You mightn't think so. That's you . . .

IRENE. How bad?

PAUL. . . . but him, now . . .

IRENE. How bad is it?

PAUL. It's bad enough . . .

> LIZ *enters with a jumper in her hand. She throws it to* PAUL.

LIZ. Here.

PAUL. . . . for him.

LIZ. Who's this?

PAUL (*putting on jumper*). The copper's wife.

LIZ. You're his wife.

PAUL. He didn't come home last night and she's worried.

LIZ. Oh, God.

PAUL. We don't know where he went. (*Turns back to his model ship, begins examining pieces, etc.*)

LIZ. Sit down. Go on. Sit down. He didn't come home?

IRENE. I'm getting worried.

LIZ. He's . . . Your husband . . .

IRENE. Yes.

LIZ. Sit down. (IRENE *sits.*) He's a policeman. Why should you be worried about him if he's a policeman?

IRENE. He might . . .

LIZ. That's it. I mean, if he's a policeman . . .

IRENE. He might do something.

LIZ. What might he do? Don't be afraid.

IRENE. I'm afraid for him.

LIZ. You're . . . Okay. I'm listening, you're afraid.

IRENE. Yes.

LIZ. You're afraid, you're alone. All right. You're alone, you've got a problem, your husband's missing, you need someone to talk to.

IRENE. No. I nee . . .

LIZ. I'm here, you can talk to me, a cup of tea?

IRENE. No thanks. I'm not really . . .

LIZ. Okay. Tell us where he usually goes. We can sort this out.

IRENE. Em . . .

LIZ. Where does he usually go?

IRENE. He usually . . . I don't . . .

LIZ. If you tell us that, then. If we know where he goes usually . . .

IRENE. Yes, he . . . (*Pause.*)

LIZ. Well?

IRENE. When?

LIZ. What?

IRENE. When? He usually comes home to me.

LIZ. When he's upset?

IRENE. He usually comes home to me.

LIZ. I'm going to make us a cup of tea. (*She exits to kitchen. Returns.*) You've someone to talk to, now. You've a problem, you've someone to talk to, a confidante, a cup of tea. Nice?

IRENE. Em . . .

LIZ. Nice? (*Pause.*)

IRENE. Yeah.

LIZ. Nice. What are you afraid of? I'm Liz.

IRENE. Irene.

LIZ. Nice to meet you. (*Of* PAUL.) Don't mind him. Tell me what you're afraid of. He won't come back?

IRENE. I don't know.

LIZ. He'll come back.

PAUL (*of ship*). Ah . . .! Jaysus!

LIZ. Don't mind him.

IRENE. Are you sure . . .? He didn't . . .?

LIZ. I don't think so. Paul?

PAUL (*of ship*). Fucking hell.

LIZ. Paul!

PAUL. What!

LIZ. He didn't say where he was going?!

PAUL. Are you making tea?

LIZ. I'm making a pot. If you want some you can get it
    yourself. Did he say where he was going?

PAUL (*pause*). I'll make myself some coffee.

LIZ. Bit of domestic strife, Irene. Paul!

PAUL. Who!

LIZ. Irene's husband. The gard.

PAUL. I don't know. No. Have we coffee?

LIZ. A fair bit of drink was consumed here last night, Irene.

IRENE. Really?

LIZ. A fair bit. We're all a bit . . .

PAUL. This thing's impossible.

LIZ. You can have a cup of tea and afterwards you can ring
    home, see if he's come back.

IRENE. Okay.

LIZ. That sound all right?

IRENE. Yeah.

LIZ. Good. (*Exits to kitchen. Pause.*)

IRENE (*to* PAUL). Are . . .?

PAUL. Mmm?

IRENE. My husband.

PAUL. Don't talk to me.

LIZ (*off-stage*). Don't talk to him. He's in the bad books.

PAUL. My bum hip's at me.

LIZ (*off-stage*). Your what?

PAUL. This thing's impossible, Liz.

LIZ (*entering with tea*). A child.

IRENE. Is he your husband?

LIZ. You must be joking.

IRENE. Whose . . .?

LIZ. Upstairs. She'd a harder night than the rest of us, God bless her. That right, Paul? (*To* IRENE.) A hard old night. (*To* PAUL.) Paul!

PAUL. Did you see the dip in that couch?

There is a knock on the door. LIZ *goes to answer it.*

WILLY. Hello.

LIZ. Ah! Your wife's here. Come in.

WILLY. My wife?!

IRENE. Willy? (*They enter.*)

PAUL. The man who shot Liberty Valence.

IRENE. Willy. I'm worried stiff, where were you?

WILLY. Thinking.

LIZ. Would you like a cup of tea, Willy?

WILLY. No thanks.

LIZ. Have a cup of tea.

IRENE. Thinking where?

WILLY. I spent the night at the station.

LIZ. Told you there was nothing to worry about.

IRENE. Ah, Willy.

WILLY. I needed to be on my own.

LIZ. You might as well . . .

IRENE. You should have rang.

LIZ. Cup of . . .?

WILLY. I didn't want to talk to anyone. I went up to the
station, had a few cups of coffee . . . It was quiet up there. I
sat at my desk and just . . . just had a long, hard think.
(*Pause.*)

LIZ (*pouring tea*). You might as well have a cup of tea.

IRENE. And where did you sleep?

WILLY. On my desk.

IRENE. Ah, Willy.

WILLY. It's good for the back.

PAUL. It is.

WILLY. Flat surface.

PAUL. Flat. Yep.

WILLY. I've slept worse places.

LIZ. Well, he's back now, anyway. Sit down, Willy.

WILLY. Sorry to be back again.

LIZ. It's alright. Sit. (*He sits.*)

WILLY. Sorry for disturbing you.

LIZ. No bother. Sugar?

WILLY. No thanks.

LIZ. There's the milk.

IRENE. Doctor Kielty called, Willy.

WILLY. That's nice of him, now, Irene.

IRENE. He wanted to know why you weren't at home.

WILLY. That's nice of him. And was he using his RTE newsreader accent?

IRENE. He wa . . .

WILLY. On the phone, it was probably his normal one, was it?

IRENE. I don't remember.

WILLY. Then again, he was talking in a professional capacity, so . . .

IRENE. He said you were suffering from post . . . Something related to shooting. Post shooting something.

WILLY. I have to do something.

IRENE. Post, related to . . .

WILLY. I thought we could have a chat.

IRENE. Related to trauma.

WILLY (*to* PAUL). I thought we could have a chat.

LIZ. I don't think he's in the humour.

IRENE. I think you shou . . . Willy!

WILLY. What?

IRENE. I think you should come with me.

LIZ. Paul?

PAUL. I'm not in the humour. (*Goes out to make coffee.*)

IRENE. He said you're suffering from . . . Let's go home. He said he needs you to call in today.

WILLY. Don't know if I'll be able to, Irene. May not be able to.

IRENE. Why not?

WILLY. May not be able to.

IRENE. What's up with you, Willy?

WILLY. Nothing's up with me, Irene. I'm just saying I may not be able to.

IRENE. Why not? (PAUL *enters.*)

WILLY (*to* PAUL). I've a proposition for you.

PAUL. I'm busy. (*Sits at ship.*)

IRENE. Why won't you be able to, Willy?

LIZ. Drink your tea, Willy.

PAUL (*of ship*). Where'd you get this bloody thing, Liz?

LIZ. Tell us your proposition, Willy.

WILLY. I can only tell it to Paul. Paul.

PAUL. What?

WILLY. Can I just . . .?

PAUL. Fucking hell!

WILLY. It'll take me just, that's all, two minutes.

PAUL. All right. Tell me it.

WILLY. Ah, now, we ca . . . The women'll have to step outside.

IRENE. Why?

WILLY. It has to be private between him and myself.

LIZ. Ah, well if that's the case . . .

IRENE. Why can't we hear?

WILLY. Irene!

LIZ. All right, Irene, they want to go mano a mano, head to head, let's go inside. C'mon, two's company.

IRENE. What happened to sharing?

WILLY. I'll share with you after.

LIZ. Irene? They need privacy.

IRENE. I'm going home.

LIZ. Sure you can stay here. We'll go inside, have a yap.

IRENE. I'm going home to our son, Willy.

WILLY. Go on home to Tommo.

IRENE. What the hell are you up to? And sleeping on your
desk? What are you up to? I need you to . . . I need you . . .
What are you doing here with these people?

WILLY. I'll see you after.

IRENE. Why won't you be able to call in to Doctor Kielty.

WILLY. Not 'Won't'. Just may not be.

IRENE. Why not?

WILLY. Not not. May not.

IRENE. Tell me what's going on, Willy.

WILLY. I'll see you after, Irene.

IRENE. Do you not trust me? (*Pause.*)

WILLY. No. (*Pause.* IRENE *heads for the front door.*)

IRENE. I'll be at home if you want me. Willy?

WILLY. Right. You'll be at home. (IRENE *leaves.*)

LIZ. There's no need for that, now.

PAUL. You right, Liz? Come on.

LIZ. No need at all. That's no way to talk. (*Exits up stairs.*)

PAUL. I hope you're not gonna start your boasting, now.

WILLY. No. I was in the station last night, there was a copy of
last night's Echo. Did you read it?

PAUL. No.

WILLY. There was an article, this woman, professor of . . .

PAUL. I don't read that shite. I read Genius . . .

WILLY. Professor of . . .

PAUL. . . . Tony Kelly. That's it. I don't know how you can
read those fucking eejits.

WILLY. The emotion professor. You know her?

PAUL. I know her. I don't read her.

WILLY. Solves problems.

PAUL. Seen her picture, she's a dog.

WILLY. A woman wrote in, her boyfriend had cheated on her, they were fighting all the time because of it, so the emotion professor told her, this was her advice, get out and sleep with someone else.

PAUL. Do the same thing.

WILLY. Balances things, makes her feel equal. Got me thinking . . .

PAUL. That was her advice?

WILLY. Yeah.

PAUL. Jesus!

WILLY. So . . . (*Pause.*)

PAUL. So . . .? (WILLY *takes out a pistol and puts it on the table.*) Jesus! Is that real?

WILLY. I need it for my proposition.

PAUL. Jesus!

WILLY. All right?

PAUL. Is it real?

WILLY. Yes. Now. You ready?

PAUL. That's a . . .

WILLY. Yes. It's a gun. This article got me thinking. I want you to shoot me.

PAUL. What?

WILLY. Do the same thing to me as I did to you.

PAUL. Shoot you.

WILLY. What I did to you. Then we're quits. Like the emotion professor says. Balance things out so it won't be between us any more. Do the same thing to me.

PAUL. Twice.

WILLY. Twi . . . (*Pause.*) If you, yeah, if you want. I don't
want you to kill me, now. Shoot me. You can shoot me in
the leg, the hip, like yourself, the arm . . .

PAUL. Is it loaded?

WILLY. It will be when you do it. Bit of balancing out.

PAUL. Some action.

WILLY. Bit of action to settle things. You shoot me instead of
printing about the . . . You know, what I . . .

PAUL. You pissing yourself like a baby.

WILLY (*beat*). Yeah.

PAUL. Can I hold it?

WILLY. Get the feel of it.

PAUL (*picking it up*). Heavy.

WILLY. Yep. (PAUL *aims the gun at various objects in the
room.*) Well?

PAUL. It's tempting, I can tell you.

WILLY. Then do it and solve all our problems. I'm sick of this
inaction.

PAUL (*putting gun down*). And get arrested.

WILLY. Sure how will you get arrested if we keep our mouths
shut? All we've to do is get rid of the evidence, clean up the
blood, get rid of the gun. You drive me close to the hospital,
my car, we'll dump the gun in the river on the way. I don't
know who shot me, I didn't get a look, someone I arrested.
Long as we keep out mouths shut, who's gonna know?

PAUL. It's tempting.

WILLY (*taking out silencer*). Got this so it's quiet, who's
gonna know? I saw enough of the bloke to know he wasn't
limping, so how could it be you? Put something under me
to collect any blood, we fuck that in the river as well.

PAUL. It's fucking tempting.

WILLY. Did you tell anyone yet?

PAUL. About . . .

WILLY. Yeah.

PAUL. No.

WILLY. Your wife?

PAUL. No.

WILLY. 'Cos if we do this, we're quits. You shooting me cancels out you telling on me.

PAUL. Yeah. No. Nobody knows yet.

WILLY. So, come on. (*Pause.*) I made you a cripple.

PAUL. Yeah.

WILLY. I shot you.

PAUL. If I . . .

WILLY. Twice. I know you want to. Do this and promise me that's the end of it. Revenge.

PAUL. There's . . . You're tempting me, Pal.

WILLY. An eye for an eye.

PAUL. You're tempting me.

WILLY. Let's see if you've got what it takes to put a bullet in someone.

PAUL. Oh, I could do it.

WILLY. See if you're man enough.

PAUL. I'm man enough to take it.

WILLY. But are you man enough to dish it out?

PAUL. More man than you.

WILLY. Well, I'm man enough to take it.

PAUL. Well, then I'm man enough to dish it out.

WILLY. Well, then, show me, then. Show me and we're quits. Even things up, do the deed, do this. (*Pause.*) Do it.

PAUL *picks up the gun, aims it at the audience.*

PAUL. All right. Yeah.

WILLY. Yeah?

PAUL. Yeah.

WILLY. All right. (*Begins loading the gun.*) Okay if we do it here?

PAUL. 'Course.

WILLY. Kid's at home.

PAUL. How old's the kid?

WILLY. Kid's six.

PAUL. Nice. (*Pause.*) Young one?

WILLY. Youngfella. (*Pause.*) Get this fucking thing over with, yeah?

PAUL. Settle it.

WILLY. Exactly.

PAUL. Done?

WILLY. You'll have to get rid of them.

PAUL. Oh, that's right, yeah. (*Calling.*) Liz?!! (*To* WILLY.) Hang on a sec'. (*Calling.*) Liz!!

LIZ *enters with* PAUL*'s stick.* WILLY *puts gun in pocket.*

LIZ. How's it going?

PAUL. We're having a good chat.

LIZ. So our peace talks are coming to fruition?

PAUL. Yeah.

LIZ. Brilliant. Here. (*Throws him stick.*)

PAUL. Where'd you find it?

LIZ (*to* WILLY). And you're mean. Don't think I'm talking to you yet, speaking to your wife like that.

PAUL. Where'd you find it?

LIZ. Upstairs.

PAUL. How's Adele?

LIZ. Not good, Paul.

PAUL (*to* WILLY). My trusty stick.

LIZ. Bit upset.

PAUL. I wasn't upstairs last night.

LIZ. Well, that's where I found it.

PAUL. Do youse want to go out to the pub?

LIZ. Well, do youse? A drink, the right atmosphere, a serious discussion . . .

PAUL. No, we'd prefer to . . .

LIZ. Drink and an old chin wag?

PAUL. We'd actually prefer to stay here, Liz.

LIZ. We're fine here.

PAUL. Well, we'd actually . . .

LIZ. Youse go down. The right atmosphere, neutral ground, pints instead of shorts . . .

PAUL. The atmosphere's grand here, Liz.

LIZ. I don't know if Adele's in the right shape.

PAUL. Nice hot whiskey, get her, huh? Do the trick. Adele likes the old hot whiskeys with the clove things. Willy and myself need to . . . Don't we?

WILLY. Need to . . .

PAUL. But why not you two . . .?

WILLY. . . . to . . . here's the right . . .

PAUL. It is. D'you know what I mean, Liz?

LIZ. I don't, Paul.

PAUL. 'Cos, like, if youse go down to the pub . . . (*There is a pounding on the door.*) Who the fff . . .? (LIZ *exits to answer it.*)

THERESA. Liz! I'm sorry it happened, but I'm scared. (THERESA *enters,* LIZ *behind her.*) Paul! I've no-one else to turn to. They came, they came back last night, I'm on my own.

LIZ. They came back?

THERESA. Last night. I heard noises. I can't stay there on my own again.

PAUL. I'm a bit tied up, Theresa.

LIZ. You're hearing things.

THERESA. No, Liz.

LIZ. Are you sure?

THERESA. Paul. I'm sorry. They were . . .

WILLY. Who's this?

THERESA. Who . . .? You're here again. You're a gard, aren't you?

PAUL. Theresa, we're a bit busy.

THERESA. You're that same bloke who . . .?

WILLY. Yes.

THERESA. Why can't you do anything? You shot him so why can't you protect me? Why can't you catch these people?

LIZ. Sit down there, Theresa.

THERESA. I'm scared, Paul. I'm sorry.

PAUL. What about your dog?

THERESA. Toby's . . . Against thieves?

LIZ. Theresa.

THERESA. Against bandits and murderers? (*To* WILLY.) You bastard, you're all alike. (*To others.*) And rapists? Toby doesn't give a fuck about me anyway. You said so yourself, Liz, the professor said. He'll leave me to these, these villains. (*To* WILLY.) Do you know what it's like to have someone break into your own domain? To have them prowling around while you're helpless asleep? They could've cut my throat. They could've had their wicked . . . I feel violated, I feel . . .

LIZ. Theresa. Relax. Talk rationally, if you sit down . . .

THERESA (*to* PAUL). I was violated and you don't care. Do you know how that feels?

WILLY. I do.

THERESA. What? You . . .? No, you don't.

WILLY. I'm being violated the same way. Of course I know how it feels. Privacy. I'm going through . . .

THERESA. But you don't know.

PAUL. Violated?!

WILLY. Yes, I do know. Privacy?

THERESA. You're a gard. How can you?

PAUL. Fucking violated?!!

WILLY. But I do.

THERESA. How can you?

PAUL. Fucking violation, you're talking about?!!! I'll tell you a few, one or two facts about violation. Violation's a bullet entering your body, piercing your skin and pushing its way inside you. Inside where it shouldn't be. Tearing through your flesh and shattering your bone and pushing its way right inside you. That's violation. Youse havent a clue what you're talking about. (ADELE *enters, stands in doorway.*) What kind of a bullet was it?

WILLY. Thirty-eight calibre.

PAUL. Through my hip, missed the socket by millimetres, came out my arse. Another one through my pelvis, lodged inside me, had to be taken out. Someone broke into your fucking house? Try taking a bullet sometime, youse wimps! Youse're all so fucking sorry for yourselves, well what about *me*?

ADELE. What about me? (*Pause.*)

PAUL. What about you? You don't know what it is either.

LIZ. Paul!

PAUL. Get over it. I got over this.

LIZ. Paul! There's no need for that!

PAUL. Should try taking a bullet sometime. (*Pause.*)

ADELE. Get out of here, Theresa.

THERESA. Someone broke into my house again, Adele.

ADELE. Did you not invite them into your bed, you tramp?

THERESA. I'm . . . I'm . . . You're the ones who . . . who've always . . .

ADELE. Get out, you fucking tart, you. I won't let you get away with this, I'm not taking this. Go home to your fucking dog . . .

THERESA. Adele!

LIZ. Adele, calm it.

ADELE. The smell off her, Liz. Do you know you stink of dog? Do you know you've the smell of a dog in fucking heat off you? No wonder you've no friends.

LIZ. Ah, Adele, now.

ADELE. Get out of my house, the stink of you. The stink. Go to your dirty mutt, fucking, your moulting fucking . . . mongrel, dirty hairs all over you. He's the only one who'll love you.

THERESA. Paul!

ADELE. He's the only one who'll love you, my husband has nothing to say to you. Go to your doggie.

LIZ. Go on, Theresa. I'll drop over later to check up on you.

ADELE. What?

LIZ. Go on, now.

THERESA. I'm afraid, Liz.

LIZ. This is a bad time.

THERESA. I'm alone.

ADELE. She's her dog.

LIZ. I'll drop over to you.

THERESA. I'm scared.

LIZ. I'll knock six times and shout 'Geronimo' in the letterbox.

THERESA. Will you?

LIZ. I will.

THERESA. Geronimo?

LIZ. Six knocks and Geronimo.

ADELE (*screaming*). GET OUT!

THERESA. Paul?

ADELE. Come on. (*Walks* THERESA *to front door and puts her out.*) Out! (*She comes back in.*)

PAUL. Jaysus! (*Beat.*) You all right? (*Pause.*) Listen, do you and Liz want to go down to the . . . pub, have a bit of a . . .

ADELE. I hate you.

PAUL. . . . hot whiskey with the . . .

LIZ. Ah, now, Adele.

ADELE. No, Liz. No. And you dropping over to her?

LIZ. Well, she's . . .

ADELE. She's bad.

LIZ. . . . she's scared, she's alone. I thought . . .

ADELE. I'm fucking alone. (*To* PAUL.) You're not the only person lives in this house. You're not the only person has it hard. We're supposed to help each other. We're husband and wife, we're . . . I'm not taking it any more, we're supposed to help each other.

PAUL. And we are.

ADELE. You're helping yourself. You're helping yourself to the fucking . . . what's her . . .?

LIZ. Theresa.

ADELE. . . . the smelly woman. The doggy woman.

PAUL. You know it's hard for me, Adele.

ADELE. You big baby. (*Pause.*) You're such a baby.

PAUL. What did you have to wear that gear for?

ADELE. What gear?

PAUL. The top, the sexy stuff, was that a joke?

ADELE. What?

PAUL. Parading yourself in front of me.

ADELE. What's that got to do with her?

PAUL. Theresa?

ADELE. Why were you seeing her?

PAUL. I was horny. (*Pause.*) You know? (*Pause.*)

ADELE. But you know I'm not able to.

LIZ. Able to what?

PAUL. Of course you're able to. I'm your husband.

ADELE. You spoke to the doctor.

LIZ. Able to what? What's this now?

ADELE. You know I'm sick.

LIZ. Do I know this?

ADELE. You told me you understood. You told me it was okay.

PAUL. Well, I don't.

ADELE. You promised me.

PAUL. I know I did.

ADELE. You said you understood.

PAUL (*shouting*). Well, I don't understand. All you've to do is spread your legs!!! All you've to do is spread your fucking legs for your husband!!! For your man!!! That's all you've to fucking do!!!

ADELE. I . . . I . . . If I . . .

PAUL. Buying me a ship to pass the time?

ADELE. . . . Paul . . .

PAUL. You open your legs, that's all there is fuckin' to it. Is that so fucking hard?!!! I've to go off with the dog lady.

LIZ. Adele.

ADELE. Need . . . I need . . .

PAUL. Is that so fucking hard to do?

LIZ. What do you need?

PAUL. With the fucking dog lady.

ADELE. Need to . . . Just, if you gimme . . . I need . . .

LIZ. Adele. (ADELE *runs upstairs*.) Adele! (LIZ *runs upstairs*.)

PAUL (*to* WILLY). Are we right?

WILLY. What?

PAUL. We right? Let's go. You got the gun?

WILLY. But your wife . . .

PAUL. We right?

WILLY. Right for what?

PAUL. For this. Are we right? The gun. Come on. Gimme the gun.

WILLY. But they're still . . .

PAUL. Fuck them. You want to do it, we're doing it now, come on, give it to me.

LIZ (*off-stage*). Adele!

WILLY. You sure? Is there something . . .?

PAUL. Do you want to do this? Come on, we've to do it now. If we don't do it now, we're not fucking doing it.

WILLY (*attaching silencer to gun*). Just wait 'til I . . .

PAUL. Hurry up. Gimme. (*Takes gun. LIZ comes downstairs and runs into kitchen. Hurried. Distressed.*) She all right? (*LIZ comes out with ADELE's pills and runs up the stairs.*) Liz! (*To WILLY.*) Right. What do I do?

WILLY. Cock it.

PAUL. Right. I know that. There bullets in it?

WILLY. Is your wife okay?

PAUL. She's fine. What next, is it loaded?

WILLY. Where do you want me to stand?

PAUL. Stand there. (*Goes to kitchen, comes back with towel.*)

WILLY. Are you sure she's okay?

PAUL. Happens all the time. Stand there. (*Throws WILLY the towel.*)

WILLY. What's going on?

PAUL. Are we doing it or what?

WILLY. We are.

PAUL. Well, come on, well.

WILLY. I'd prefer if you did it quickly.

PAUL (*pause*). Hold your horses.

PAUL *begins spreading newspapers on the floor.* WILLY *helps him.*

LIZ (*off*). Paul!

WILLY. Aim it, by the way, when you're aiming it, aim it a couple of inches below your target because there's a kick and it can throw you off, okay? Don't want you hitting me in the wrong place.

PAUL (*pointing at newspaper*). Know who that is?

WILLY. Yeah.

PAUL. Who?

WILLY. Tony Kelly.

PAUL. Genius.

WILLY. You'll get me to the hospital?

PAUL. I'll drive you straight after. Just let me get my . . . (*Deep breath.*) Okay.

LIZ (*off-stage*). Paul?!

PAUL. Okay. (WILLY*'s looking upstairs.*) Willy? Willy, are we doing this?

WILLY. Yeah.

PAUL. Where do you want it?

WILLY. The leg, the hip, just not the middle.

PAUL. Right.

WILLY. Or the head.

PAUL. The leg or the hip.

WILLY. The leg or the hip.

PAUL. Well, pick. Which?

WILLY. What?

PAUL. The hip or the leg?

WILLY. Oh. The leg.

PAUL. The leg.

WILLY. Is it properly cocked?

PAUL (*cocking it*). Yep.

WILLY. All right, go. The leg, is it?

PAUL. Yeah.

WILLY. All right, go. (PAUL *aims.*)

LIZ (*off-stage*). Adele? (*Pause. Louder.*) Adele?! (*Pause. Hysterical.*) Adele!! Adele!!

PAUL (*lowering gun*). Just gimme a second.

WILLY. Aim carefully.

LIZ (*off-stage*). Adele! Paul!

PAUL. Just give me a second or two. Have to . . . work myself up.

WILLY. Take your time.

PAUL. Just give me a minute.

LIZ (*off-stage*). Paul!

PAUL. You've never been shot before.

WILLY. I'm about to.

PAUL. It hurts.

WILLY. Well, come on, then.

PAUL. Hold your horses. (*Pause. Aims gun.*) You all tensed up?

WILLY. Yeah.

PAUL. The right leg, right?

WILLY. The right one.

PAUL. You right?

WILLY. Thanks for not telling them. About the . . .

PAUL. Forget about it. I'm not your friend.

WILLY. I know you're not.

LIZ (*off-stage*). Paul!!

PAUL. Good. Are you right? (*Pause.*)

WILLY. Okay. Two inches lower.

PAUL. Two inches. Right. (*Pause.*)

WILLY. Ready? (*Pause.*)

PAUL. Yeah. (*Long pause.*)

LIZ (*off-stage*). PAUL!!!

WILLY (*almost simultaneously*). GO!!!

 Blackout.

THE ASPIDISTRA CODE

Characters

JOE

DRONGO

BRENDAN

SONIA

CRAZY HORSE

RONNIE

An average sized living room. A couple of armchairs on either side of a coffee table. Television, down left. Large window at back and a few feet in front, a sofa. At left, a hallway leading to the front door. At right, a doorway leading to kitchen. Beside this doorway, a phone on the wall. Down right, a dining table and chairs. Sitting at this table are JOE *and* BRENDAN. *There are playing cards scattered across the table.* BRENDAN *is picking them up and putting the deck back together.*

JOE. Imagine, right? We're in a . . . One of those . . . Say, for instance, you're . . . (BRENDAN *tries to interrupt.*) No. Hang on. Hang on. You're in . . . Hold your horses. Say you're in Las Vegas, right?

BRENDAN. No, no . . .

JOE. You're in Vegas, playing at one of those crap tables. Or a . . . No. You're playing cards. (BRENDAN *tries to interrupt.*) Stop it, will you? You're at the card table and you're playing for high stakes against James Bond and a Venetian, say, property dealer and the . . . Who else? All these rich fuckers. The Duke of . . . The Duke of Venice. Hang on. The Duke of Venice and his six muscley bodyguards. They look like the Chippendales, only with tuxedos, right? You're playing for chips. This is just for instance, now. You've a tuxedo as well.

BRENDAN. Tuxedo?

JOE. This'd be the class of people you're playing against. They're all rich fuckers, all right? Now, you lose the game and you lose all your chips. That's all you had and now it's gone. You've nothing. Now, you're safe enough. You're not lacking for a place to stay or anything, you're booked in somewhere. *But* . . . That's all you have. *Now* . . . You get a yen for something, I don't know. For a glass of wine or champagne. You want something to eat.

BRENDAN. Cigarettes.

JOE. Right. We'll say cigarettes. You have a yen for a smoke. The excitement. You know the way, sometimes, like after a good game, you fancy a smoke.

BRENDAN. Yeah.

JOE. And, you're broke, now. So what are you going to do? Are you going to go up to the Ayotollah of, of fucking Iraq . . .? for a few quid, a few dollars for twenty cigarettes? You can't get tens there. Of money of what he just won from you? Because if you do that, all you're saying is, effectively, like, gimme some of my money back. Is he going to give you something?

BRENDAN. No.

JOE. That he just won off you? 'Cos he won it. The rules are strict. It's not yours any more, it's his.

BRENDAN. I know.

JOE. Is he going to return some of your, which is now his, money to you?

BRENDAN. Of course not.

JOE. Probably have you thrown out of the place or something. Get one of his Chippendales to give you a good hiding.

BRENDAN. Mmm.

JOE. Do you see? (*Pause.*)

BRENDAN. What if . . .

JOE (*interrupting*). No, no, no . . .

BRENDAN. He could be a nice bloke.

JOE. No, Bren. It's not like that. It doesn't work that way. He probably is a nice bloke and all. Most people are. Thing is . . . What I'm trying to get across to you . . . Do you understand?

BRENDAN. Yeah.

JOE. You . . .

BRENDAN. I understand.

JOE. It's against the rules to give you money back. Even if he wanted to throw you a few . . . something for cigarettes. Etiquette demands that he refrain from such, you know, shows of emotion or good fellowship. And that's the rules. He can't do it if he takes his gambling seriously. We all do. We have to. And if you're going to take it seriously, you have to follow the rules. Do you think I'm greedy? 'Cos I'm trying to make you understand I'm not. Ciga . . . Something small even. It doesn't matter the size of the thing. I have to obey the etiquette of the table.

Pause. JOE *leans back in his chair and lights a cigarette.* BRENDAN *watches.*

BRENDAN. Play another hand.

JOE. With what? You've none left. And we're not playing for money.

BRENDAN. Play for 10ps.

JOE. No, Bren. No money. The game's over. Sorry that has to be the way, but . . . Money's out. We've what? (*Looks at watch.*) Half an hour. Relax. (*Pause.*)

BRENDAN. Half an hour.

JOE. Relax. (*Pause.*) What are you worried about?

BRENDAN. A lot of things.

JOE. Relax. (*Pause.*)

BRENDAN. I'm . . .

JOE. Relax.

BRENDAN. Who knows . . .? You see, who knows what way it's going to go?

JOE. Nobody knows, so relax. (*Pause.*)

BRENDAN. Anything could . . .

JOE (*interrupting*). Hey, hey, fuck's sake, we've got the Crazy Horse, haven't we. All right, you're nervous, but we . . .

Whatever happens with him, we can . . . Even the worst isn't going to be that bad, all right? Calm down. So calm down and relax. Take it easy.

BRENDAN. Okay. (BRENDAN *shuffles the cards. Pause.*)

JOE. Bit of trivia, Bren.

BRENDAN. What?

JOE. English, right . . .?

BRENDAN. Yeah?

JOE. . . . the language, contains twice or more, I don't remember, as many words as a language, say, like French.

BRENDAN. Twice, yeah?

JOE. Or more. (*Pause.*)

BRENDAN. So, English would be a fairly hard language to learn. If you had to learn it. Say, if you were foreign.

JOE. Oh, definitely. Definitely. (*Pause.*)

BRENDAN. So, there's . . . Are there things the French don't have a word for?

JOE. No, they've a word for almost everything. Maybe you wouldn't think so.

BRENDAN. Yeah.

JOE. They don't have as *many* words. But the words they *do* have are better put to use. D'you know what I mean? For example, one word might have anything from fifty to a hundred meanings, depending on which way you say it.

BRENDAN. Pronunciation.

JOE. Yeah. Or what context. You say something with a deep voice and it means something completely different from the exact same word. Exact same. Same spelling, everything, only . . .

BRENDAN (*interrupting*). Wait, wait, listen. (*Pause. They listen.*)

JOE. What?

We hear footsteps descending stairs.

BRENDAN. Sonia. (*Looks at watch.*) Shite!

JOE. What?

BRENDAN. Supposed to . . . (SONIA *enters.*) Hey, hey!

SONIA (*sleepily*). Hey.

BRENDAN. All right?

SONIA. MmmHmm.

BRENDAN. We were playing cards.

SONIA. It's okay. What time is it? (*Yawns.*)

BRENDAN. Almost twenty to. We were . . . Got a bit caught up. Sorry. (*To* JOE.) How long was it?

JOE. A while, Bren. Good game it was.

BRENDAN (*to* SONIA). How are you feeling?

SONIA. Bit sleepy. Tea?

BRENDAN (*getting up quickly*). No, no, no. Sit down, sit down.

He hustles her towards an armchair.

Get you a cup of . . . (*To* JOE.) Tea, Joe?

JOE. I wouldn't say no, Bren.

BRENDAN (*to* SONIA). Sit down. You're staggering around like a . . . Sit. (*She sits.*) Good. (*Exiting to kitchen.*) I'll get it.

Silence.

JOE. You know something, Sonia?

SONIA. What?

JOE. The French language, beautiful and all as it is, contains only half as many words as English.

SONIA (*not really interested*). Really?

JOE. They've got no word for the word 'Splash.' If they want to say splash, they have to say something like, 'The sound that water makes when something hard hits it.' Hard to believe, isn't it.

SONIA. Mmm.

JOE. Or they could go 'Pffshhh!'

SONIA (*absently*). They could. (*Pause.*)

JOE. Why don't you go next door?

SONIA (*suddenly coming to life*). No, I . . . Joe! No. Brendan and I already spoke about this.

JOE. But this isn't your business. Well, it is your business, it's your house and all, but it's not, like . . .

SONIA (*interrupting*). I'm not going next door.

JOE. You should go in and sit down and have . . . (*Sighs.*) It's not really your business being here. Not business. That's not . . . But, you know . . .

SONIA. Joe. I'm not going next door. We . . . We . . .

JOE. You shouldn't be here.

SONIA. . . . we already spoke about this, Joe. The discussion's over. It happened before you got here. I'm staying with my husband.

JOE. This isn't for ladies.

SONIA. This isn't for anyone.

JOE. *Particularly* for ladies. I don't want to see you . . . I want to shield you from things your eyes shouldn't be, you know, tainted with. You're not doing yourself any good.

SONIA. Don't worry about me.

JOE (*casually*). Oh, I'm not. (*Then, seriously.*) Come one, Sonia. (*Imitates her.*) 'Don't worry about me.' You know what that is? You know what you're doing there . . .?

The telephone rings. JOE *leaps up.*

I'll get it, I'll get it, let me get it. Could be . . . (*Picks up.*) Hello? (*Pause.*) Yes. Just hold the line one moment, please.

JOE *holds the phone out for* SONIA. *She takes it from him and he sits back down. As* SONIA *speaks,* BRENDAN *peeks his head in the door and aims a quizzical look at* JOE. JOE *shakes his head.* BRENDAN *disappears back into the kitchen.*

SONIA (*into phone*) Hello? No, everything's fff . . . No, we should . . . He's . . . (*Pause.*) No, thanks a lot, no. I'm sure. (*Pause.*) No, I'll . . . No, really. Thanks a lot all the same. Yeah, thanks a lot. (*Pause.*) Okay. (*Pause.*) All right, byebye. (*She hangs up. To* JOE.) I don't know.

JOE. Why do you talk to her?

SONIA. I don't know. Ah, she . . . (*Pause.*)

JOE. What did she want?

SONIA. She wanted to know if she could be of any assistance. Was there anything I needed.

JOE. About what?

SONIA (*sitting back down*). What?

JOE. About this?

SONIA. She asked me if . . . Yeah. She was offering . . .

JOE. Why? 'Cos of this?

SONIA. She . . . Yeah. Why else?

JOE. Ah, Sonia.

SONIA. She was only . . .

JOE. You told her.

SONIA. Yes.

JOE. Ah, Sonia.

SONIA. What?

JOE. That wasn't the best of moves, now.

SONIA. It's Karen. What's the problem?

JOE. You just said you don't like her.

SONIA (*pause*). Right.

JOE. So, why are you going around telling her what's going on?

SONIA. I'm not 'going around.'

JOE. You *told* her.

   Enter BRENDAN.

BRENDAN. Who was that?

SONIA. Karen. The phone? Karen.

BRENDAN. Karen?

JOE. She knows.

BRENDAN. Who's Karen?

SONIA. Karen next door.

JOE. She knows.

BRENDAN. Knows this? What does she know?

JOE. About this. That was her.

BRENDAN. On the phone.

JOE. Asking if she could be of assistance. (*Pause.*)

BRENDAN. Who? (*To* SONIA.) Sonia!

SONIA. I told her yesterday. I'm sorry, but I told her. What difference can it make? The only difference is she wants to help. At least she gives a shit.

BRENDAN (*pause*). I don't like her. I'm sorry, Sonia. I know she's your friend and you like her and all . . .

SONIA. I don't like her.

BRENDAN. She's your friend.

SONIA. But I never said I liked her.

JOE. On the contrary.

BRENDAN. But the way it . . .

SONIA. I never said I liked her. (*Pause.*)

BRENDAN. So you *don't* like her.

SONIA. Not really. No. (*Pause.*)

BRENDAN. Neither do I.

JOE. Some tea, there, Bren?

BRENDAN (*remembering*). Oh, yeah.

> BRENDAN *exits to the kitchen again. He returns with a tray of tea, cups, condiments. He puts it on the dining table. They sit down and start pouring, milking, sugaring, etc. The telephone rings again.* JOE *jumps up and answers it.*

JOE (*into phone*). Hello? Hey, how are you? You, you . . . (*Pause.*) Okay. No, no, no, not at all, no. Yes, that's . . . No, that's . . . (*Short pause.*) I don't know. Whatever you want. (*Short pause.*) Yes. (*Looks at watch.*) Okay. Hurry if you can, could you? If you *can*. (*Pause.*) Okay. I'm sorry. I'll see you then. All right. Goodbye. What? (*Pause.*) No, I . . . No, I said 'Good*bye*.' Yeah. All right. See you soon. (*Hangs up. To others.*) Thought I was calling him a good boy.

BRENDAN. That him?

JOE (*imitating whoever was on phone.*) 'You patronising me?'

BRENDAN. Joe.

JOE. That was him.

BRENDAN. The Crazy Horse?!

JOE. That was the Crazy Horse.

SONIA. What did he say?

BRENDAN. Is he coming?

JOE. He'll be here soon. (*Pause.*)

BRENDAN (*to* SONIA). Why don't you go next door.

SONIA. No, Bren. I already told you I don't like her. I'm not going in there.

JOE. Why don't you just stay here.

BRENDAN. Why don't you . . .? All right, just . . . I'm worried.

SONIA. So am I.

Pause. They drink their tea contemplatively. There is a deep, foreboding silence.

SONIA. I was thinking, maybe . . .

BRENDAN. What?

SONIA. You know the chair?

JOE. Lovely tea, Bren.

SONIA. The old . . . My grandmother's chair. The chair my grandmother left me.

BRENDAN. The chair upstairs.

SONIA. It's worth money.

BRENDAN. That *chair*? That *eyesore*?

SONIA. The chair upstairs. It must be worth . . .

BRENDAN. That fucking *thing!*

SONIA. The money. We could use it, you know, to . . . You know.

BRENDAN. With the Drongo.

SONIA. Yes.

BRENDAN. It's an *eye*sore.

JOE. Which chair is this?

SONIA. It's an eyesore, I know, but he could . . . We could give it to him to sell.

BRENDAN. Where would he sell it?

SONIA. I don't know. At a market. In one of those things.

JOE. At an auction.

SONIA. At a, yeah. People could bid for it.

BRENDAN. The Drongo deals in . . . He doesn't deal in antiques. Hard cash. The Drongo is a hard cash man. What the hell would he want with a chair?

SONIA. It's an antique.

BRENDAN (*to* JOE). Will you give me a cigarette?

JOE. Sorry, Bren.

BRENDAN. Just a . . . *One*!

JOE. Bren. You know I can't. You know the rules, there's no refunds. I won these. It'd be ethically wrong. Tomorrow, maybe.

BRENDAN (*sulkily*). Tomorrow.

SONIA. I'm going to bring it down.

SONIA *exits the sitting room and goes upstairs.*

BRENDAN. Give me a cigarette.

JOE. No.

BRENDAN. I need one.

JOE *lights a cigarette for himself.*

JOE. All this talk of cigarettes. Christ. (*Pause. Exhales smoke.*) Another bit of trivia for you, right? In the future. Not in our life. In the distant future . . . There'll be a brand of cigarettes which, when we inhale, will purify our bodies' innards, and which, when we exhale, due to the mixing of the special tobacco and the oxygen in our lungs, will promote rain forest growth and ozone layer repair. (*Takes a drag on cigarette.*)

BRENDAN (*not really listening*). Imagine. (*Looks at watch.*)

JOE. Also . . . (Not tryin' to torture you or anything.) They also say that . . . You listening?

BRENDAN. Mmm.

JOE. Skyscrapers won't be made from steel and cement any more, but from foliage and, and mud and, like, things that nature has provided. They'll still be the same things; big buildings. Still serve the same uses. But they'll be built from the gifts, say, of the earth, which'll be . . . *The tobacco.* This special tobacco will enhance the growth of all good things. So, we can all smoke if we want to. And have big buildings, and . . .

BRENDAN. Very nice.

JOE. This is what they say, now. I myself . . . (Not trying to torture you, Bren.) (*Takes a long drag on his cigarette. Exhales.*) I like a good smoke.

The telephone rings again and JOE *jumps up to answer it.*

JOE (*into phone*). Hello? Is this . . . You're the . . . (*Pause.*) No, everything's fine. I'm, yes. I'm Brendan's brother. (*Pause.*) I supp . . . No, it's okay. (*Pause.*)

As JOE *speaks, we can hear something heavy bumping down the stairs.*

Listen, could . . . Yes. There's just . . . Could you please . . . Could you . . . We're waiting for an important call. (*Pause.*) Yes, so . . . (*Pause.*) Yes, *we'll* get on to *you.* (*Pause.*) Yes, we'll get on to you. Right. (*Hangs up.*)

SONIA *enters, lugging the antique chair behind her.*

SONIA. Who was that?

BRENDAN. Your 'friend.'

JOE. Jesus Christ. Look at that. Who in their right . . . Is that it?

SONIA. Yeah.

JOE. That's the chair, the . . . The special chair.

BRENDAN. The magic chair.

SONIA. The an*tique* chair. That was my grandmother's chair.

JOE. That's a travesty.

SONIA (*to* BRENDAN). Who was it? Karen?

BRENDAN. She's checking up.

SONIA. I'm not going over there.

JOE. Fuck her.

BRENDAN. Just leave it there, Sonia.

SONIA. I'll . . . It might . . .

BRENDAN. Could be.

SONIA. . . . . It might come in useful.

JOE. That's a bloody disgrace.

BRENDAN. Leave it there.

> SONIA *leaves the chair beside one of the other armchairs.*
> *It now looks like a hideous part of the sitting room*
> *furniture. She sits back down.*

Won't be long now.

> *The lights of a passing car shine through the window.*
> *Everybody stiffens. The car continues on its way. They relax.*

(*To* JOE.) What about the Crazy Horse?

JOE. What about him?

BRENDAN. Do you know him well?

JOE. I already told you, Bren.

BRENDAN. Remind us.

SONIA. Yeah.

JOE. I know he's crazy.

SONIA. Crazy?

JOE. Well, he's the Crazy Horse.

BRENDAN. But he's a friend of yours.

JOE. No, he's . . . No.

BRENDAN. Well, what is he? You *know* him.

SONIA. He's not your friend, Joe?

BRENDAN. Is he coming?

JOE. Wasn't he just on the phone, Bren.

BRENDAN. That doesn't mean he's coming.

SONIA. And you don't *know* him.

JOE. I *do* know him. He's someone I know but I wouldn't call him a *friend* of mine.

SONIA. He doesn't like you?

BRENDAN. Is he coming?

JOE. Yes. He's coming.

SONIA. Why doesn't he like you?

JOE. It's not that he doesn't *like* me. He's just not a friend of mine.

SONIA. Why not?

JOE. Because . . . I don't know. He's a bit difficult to get on with. He has problems with certain things, social things, hence his fucking . . . his occupation. His ideas are different to most people's. They're different to mine, anyway.

BRENDAN. How, different?

JOE. And that's why I don't hang around with him.

SONIA. And we're letting him in our house?

JOE. He's not . . .

BRENDAN. He's problems?

JOE. He's has a few problems. Nothing.

BRENDAN. Could he do something?

JOE. Something, what?

BRENDAN. Is he dangerous? That's what I'm . . . As Sonia said. We don't want . . .

SONIA. That's right. In the house. I mean, who knows . . .?

JOE. He's . . .

BRENDAN. Yeah. In our home. Would it be stupid?

JOE. He *is* dangerous, yes, but . . .

BRENDAN. And he's going to . . . You've . . .

JOE. He's . . .

SONIA. In our house?

JOE. He's . . . Hold your horses, for Jaysus sake, *yes*, he is
   dangerous, but he's . . . Hang on, he's a channelled, a
   controlled danger. He's on our side, for fuck's sake. He's
   coming here to help us. He's not an animal. (*Pause.*)

BRENDAN (*to* SONIA). Maybe you should go into Karen.

SONIA. Fuck off, Bren.

JOE. He's here to . . . Calm down, Bren, will you? For fuck's
   sake relax, the two of you. When I said he has problems, I
   meant he's annoying, right? He's not a monster, he's just a
   bit strange. His real name's Al, sure. I mean, the worst thing
   he'll do is get on your nerves, all right? There's no problem
   whatsoever about having him in your house. (*Pause.*) Okay?
   (*Pause.*)

BRENDAN. If you say.

JOE. I do.

SONIA (*to herself*). The Crazy Horse.

   There is a thunderous knocking on the front door.
   Everybody jumps.

BRENDAN. God!

JOE (*getting up*). Relax.

   JOE *goes out to answer the door.*

RONNIE (*off-stage*). How's it going?

JOE (*off-stage*). What's up, there, Ronnie?

RONNIE (*off-stage*). Can I come in?

JOE (*off-stage*). Yeah. Come on in.

We hear the hall door shut and JOE *and* RONNIE *enter the sitting room.* RONNIE *is from the country and speaks with a very heavy accent.*

BRENDAN. What's up, Ronnie?

RONNIE (*dejectedly*). Ah.

BRENDAN. You all right?

SONIA. What is it?

RONNIE. I . . . (*Sighs.*)

BRENDAN. What's wrong?

RONNIE. The feckin' . . . (*Pause.*) Ah, you know, I just . . . (*Pause.*)

SONIA. Ronnie?

RONNIE. Feckin' Karen! Do you know what . . .? I'm botherin' you, amen't I? You've got this thing happening and I'm in your way, amen't I?

SONIA. No.

RONNIE. 'Cos the feckin' hooer. I'm supposed to come in and see you're all right. I know you don't want, you, you don't need me here. Can't tell her that. Sent me in, she did.

BRENDAN. Do you . . . (*To* SONIA.) Get Ronnie a glass, a drink, will you, Sonia? (*To* RONNIE.) What do you want, Ronnie?

RONNIE. 'Go in, go in.' 'No,' I say. 'All right, then,' she says. 'That's it.' 'What?' says I. 'If you don't go next door, then that's a month.' D'you know what a month is?

BRENDAN. What?

RONNIE. I don't get me hole for a month. She doesn't let me, I'm sorry, Sonia, shag her for a month. This is the thing, now. This is the new business. Before . . . Last time it was dinner. Now, I'm a hard working man. I need my grub. Now it's sex. She won't . . . That's her new thing, now, for getting what she wants. Withdrawal of favours, the slut! One year we're married. Withdrawal of favours. Who the devil does she think she is? One month if I don't come in. I'm sorry. I'm supposed to be, I don't know, protecting you or something. What the hell good am I?

JOE. Exactly.

RONNIE. What the hell can I do? One month, can you believe that? Who would belie . . . (*Notices the antique chair.*) Where the hell did you get that thing? (*Pause.*)

SONIA. It's my grandmother's. Was.

JOE. It's an antique.

BRENDAN. What do you want to drink, Ronnie?

RONNIE. Would you believe it, Brendan? What would you do if . . .? A month. Four weeks. What gives her the right? Using her whatsit? Using her . . . Who gave her the right? A month of wanking, excuse me, like a thirteen year old. 'Scuse me, Sonia.

SONIA. It's all right, Ronnie.

RONNIE. Give us . . . Give us a . . . What have you got?

BRENDAN. We've got some whiskey. (*To* SONIA.) Have we whiskey?

SONIA. Paddys.

BRENDAN (*to* RONNIE). Or a nice cup of . . .

RONNIE (*interrupting*). Paddys'll do. I could use a glass. Straight. How are you, Joe? No, with ice.

JOE. How are you, Ronnie?

RONNIE. Unbelievable. That's . . . (*To* JOE.) No, but isn't it? Isn't it beyond belief? (*To* BRENDAN.) Would you believe it, Brendan?

SONIA *exits to get the drink.*

JOE. Relax, Ronnie. Calm it. Sit down. (*Pause.*) Sit down and relax. (RONNIE *sits.*) That's . . . Yeah. (*Pause.*)

RONNIE. Hooer.

JOE. Relax. (*Pause.*)

BRENDAN. Have you got a cigarette, Ronnie?

RONNIE. Suppose.

> RONNIE *gives* BRENDAN *a cigarette*. BRENDAN *looks at* JOE.

JOE. What?

BRENDAN (*lighting cigarette*). Nothing a'tall, Joe.

> SONIA *re-enters and gives* RONNIE *his whiskey*.

SONIA. There you go.

RONNIE. Thanks.

SONIA. So, how is Karen, anyway?

RONNIE. How's . . .? *Fuck* Karen!

SONIA. Ronnie. I was only . . .

RONNIE (*interrupting*). *Shag* her. Thinks she can control me. First food. Then sex. I go out and earn the bread, so I do. I earn the crust. You don't see her makin' demands of a Friday night, *do* you? On *pay* day. Pay day's be nice to Ronnie day.

JOE. What does she look like?

RONNIE. You met her before, Joe.

JOE. Did I?

RONNIE. We were over here once for . . . Remember the party you had for . . . The party Brendan and Sonia had for little Jason's communion. Where *is* Jason?

SONIA. My sister's.

RONNIE. Good idea. Keep him out of danger. (*To* JOE.) For Jason's communion. You remember her.

JOE. No, I . . .

RONNIE. We were here. Hatchetface. She was with me.

SONIA. She's not a hatchetface, Ronnie.

RONNIE. She's not. She's a good looking woman.

JOE. Yeah?

RONNIE. I have to admit, now. (*To* BRENDAN.) Brendan?

BRENDAN. Yeah, she's . . .

RONNIE. She's grand.

BRENDAN. . . . . She's an attractive woman.

RONNIE. But she's a hooer.

JOE. What was she wearing?

RONNIE. I don't know. Some yoke.

SONIA. She was wearing a brown suit.

JOE. Ah, yeah. Now, I . . . That was the night Pebbles . . .

SONIA. Oh, Jesus, yeah.

JOE. She . . .

SONIA. Yeah.

JOE. . . . He pissed on your woman's lap. Carole Stewart.

BRENDAN. Typical.

SONIA. That was funny, now . . .

JOE. Poor bitch.

SONIA. . . . wasn't it.

JOE. What was it she . . .?

SONIA. That devil dog.

JOE. That's it. 'Your devil dog.' (*To* RONNIE.) And Karen was
. . . I remember her. The brown suit.

RONNIE. Brown suit. Says something, doesn't it. A brown
power suit and the perfect colour for her.

BRENDAN. Why?

RONNIE. Colour of shite.

JOE. She doesn't drink.

RONNIE. Doesn't do anything.

SONIA. . . . So *funny*!

RONNIE. Doesn't do anything. Trying to, now . . . This is the . . .
A man can't live without a bit of drink once in a while,
now, can he?

BRENDAN. What's she . . .?

RONNIE. Yeah, she's . . .

BRENDAN. . . . she's . . .

RONNIE. Yes. That's another, the latest . . . Trying to *wean*
me. Trying to get me off, the bitch. (*To* SONIA.) I'm sorry.

SONIA. It's all right.

RONNIE (*to himself*). The hooer! (*Pause. Looks at chair.*)
That's some chair.

SONIA. That's an antique. It's worth a lot of money.

RONNIE. I'd like to ram it down her fecking gullet . . .

JOE. It's an appeasement.

RONNIE. . . . Strangle her. A what?

JOE. An appeasement.

SONIA. It's for the Drongo, Ronnie.

RONNIE. This the . . .

JOE. Yeah. They call him the Drongo.

RONNIE. What's he going to do with it?

JOE. He can sell it. Who knows? It's worth a lot of money.

RONNIE. How much?

SONIA. Over two thousand pounds.

RONNIE. Yeah? And how much do you owe?

SONIA. Six hundred and fifty.

RONNIE. He might take it. That's worth a lot of money, that chair.

JOE. Do you know that the word 'Drongo' is actually a derogatory term?

BRENDAN. Is it?

JOE. Mmm Hmm.

SONIA. Meaning?

JOE. I'm not sure. But something bad, I think.

RONNIE. A drongo.

SONIA. It means something bad?

JOE. Yeah.

SONIA. Does *he* know this?

JOE. Jesus, I don't know, but . . . (*Pause. Looks at her.*)

SONIA. Right. No. Of course.

JOE. Okay?

SONIA. Yeah.

RONNIE (*holding out empty glass*). Thanks, Sonia.

SONIA. You're welcome.

She takes the glass, but stays where she is for the time being.

JOE. Listen, Ronnie. As long as you're staying here . . .

RONNIE. No fecking choice, have I?

JOE. Right. Well, as long as you're here: When the Crazy Horse comes, could you just talk as little as possible, okay?

RONNIE. The Crazy Horse?

JOE. Just sit down and be quiet and pretend you're not here. You can't do anything to . . .

RONNIE (*interrupting*). The Crazy Horse is coming here?

JOE. Yeah.

RONNIE. Here?

JOE. Yes. (*Pause.*) You know him?

RONNIE. I heard about him.

JOE. He's a friend of mine. *Well* . . . What did you hear about him?

RONNIE. Do you know him personally?

JOE. I do.

SONIA. What did you hear, Ronnie?

RONNIE. Heard he did something to a dog once.

SONIA (*to* BRENDAN). Pebbles!

BRENDAN. Ssshh.

JOE. What did he do, Ronnie?

RONNIE. Well . . . (*Pause.*) Some fella did something on some fella. I don't know what. Something bad. So the fella that had something, the thing done to him, knew the Crazy Horse. Or knew how to get in touch with him, anyway. So, he asked him for some assistance. I think it's something like the Crazy Horse won't help you unless he feels it's . . .

JOE. To see that it's ethically right that he help you.

RONNIE. Yeah, ethically . . . yes. He won't help . . . Is that right? He won't help just anyone.

JOE. That's correct. He has to decide . . .

RONNIE. Right. If the people are deserving.

JOE. Right.

RONNIE. Anyway, this man, he decided, was. So what it was was, he was being persecuted for something and the thing was to stop the fella, you know, the other lad from persecuting him. So the Crazy Horse drops down to your man's house. This is the . . . the . . .

BRENDAN. The bloke who was doing the persecuting.

RONNIE. Yeah. The fella doing it. His house. And he kicks him around a bit and he ties him to a chair and says to him, 'Who dies?' Which I hear is a typical thing he does. 'You make the decision who dies and who lives.'

SONIA. Between who?

RONNIE. It was . . . He had to decide between his . . . This . . . What kind? A . . . A . . . The little . . .

JOE. A Jack Russell.

RONNIE. Yeah?

JOE. Yeah.

RONNIE. Little . . . The little mutt. Between . . . Or this bag of . . . This moggie. A cat he had. Now, anyone with a bit of common sense . . . Which one are you going to choose?

SONIA. The dog.

RONNIE. The d . . . To live?

SONIA. Yeah. The dog to live.

RONNIE. Right. Who the feck'd pick a cat over a dog? Cats, they're treacherous little . . . hooers. Bit of common sense, you're going to pick the dog. So he picks the dog.

JOE. And the Crazy Horse kills the dog.

RONNIE. Yeah. He lets the little ball of shite live and kills the dog.

JOE. Tell them how he does it.

BRENDAN. No, hold on. I don't think . . . (*To* SONIA.) You don't want to hear this, do you?

SONIA (*to* RONNIE). No, go on.

BRENDAN. Is this going to . . .

SONIA. I want to hear it.

BRENDAN. . . . . to upset you, or . . .?

SONIA (*to* RONNIE). What happened the dog?

RONNIE. Right. Well, first he tied your man up and taped his eyes open. Then, he put the dog in a see through plastic bag and hung it out of the light. So your man had to sit there with his eyes taped open and watch his dog suffocate. (*Pause.*) So the dog's hanging there and your man's watching it 'cos he can't do anything else. Just watch it. And the bag's going in and out, in and out, slower and slower with, you know . . . as the dog breathes. And it's getting slower and slower, in and out, in and out, slower and slower, and the man's watching it, and the bag's all fogged up, now, so all we can see is the movement of the bag, in and out, and slower and slower and slower . . . (*Pause. Then, matter of factly.*) . . . and the doggie croaked. Doggie dies and all this while, the feckin' moggie is skulking around the room and pissing on the floor while man's best friend is taking his last. Few. Breaths . . . Ever.

BRENDAN. Jesus Christ.

SONIA. Pebbles.

BRENDAN. Shut up, will you? *Fuck* Pebbles.

JOE. He's on our side, Sonia.

RONNIE. But, he's a good lad, I hear. He's decent in that he's . . . He goes around doing good deeds. He helps people less fortunate. Or the downtrodden.

SONIA *notices that she still has the empty glass in her hand. She exits with it to the kitchen.*

JOE. They say that if you die in your home, a dog will stay by your side the whole time and die with you. He'll remain loyal and true and die with his master. But a cat'll, as soon as he sees you're helpless, he'll eat you. A cat's got neither morals nor ethics.

RONNIE. Doesn't surprise me, Joe. Some women are like that, too, and I'm not talking about your Sonia, Brendan. If you know what I mean. I'm talking about someone else.

SONIA *re-enters.*

BRENDAN (*to* SONIA). He all right?

RONNIE (*half to himself*). Someone near*by*, though.

SONIA. She's asleep. Poor little thing.

BRENDAN (*nervously*). How much longer? Jesus. I just wish it was over. (*Pause.*) Get it over with. (*Pause.*)

JOE. Relax. (*Pause.*)

BRENDAN. Need a . . . (*Sighs.*) Can I have another cigarette, Ronnie?

RONNIE. Sorry, Brendan. Five left.

BRENDAN. Well, give me one, will you?

RONNIE. Five *left*, Brendan. That's all I have 'till tomorrow. I gave you one.

BRENDAN. Five, so give me one and then you'll have four.

RONNIE. Sorry, Brendan. From . . . I calculate. From now until I go to bed, I'll smoke exactly five cigarettes.

BRENDAN. Smoke four.

RONNIE. No.

JOE (*to* BRENDAN). Play him for one.

BRENDAN. With what?

JOE. I don't know, with . . . What have you got?

RONNIE. What's this, now?

BRENDAN. Emmm . . .

RONNIE. What's this? Poker?

JOE. Play him for the chair. The chair against a cigarette.

RONNIE. Poker, is it?

SONIA. That chair's an antique. (*To* BRENDAN.) And you should be more worried about the Drongo.

SONIA *exits to the kitchen.*

RONNIE. I don't normally gamble.

JOE. Karen cure of that already, Ronnie?

RONNIE. Very funny. Whatsit? Poker?

BRENDAN. Yeah. (*Pause.*)

RONNIE. What have you got?

BRENDAN. I don't know. I'll play you for . . .

JOE. Play him for the chair.

RONNIE. I don't want the chair.

BRENDAN. I've got . . . I'll play you for 10ps. 20ps. A twenty against a cigarette. (*Pause.*)

RONNIE. An aspidistra.

BRENDAN. One of *my* . . .

RONNIE. A cigarette against an aspidistra. (*Pause.*)

BRENDAN (*not too pushed on the idea*). Ehhmm . . .

JOE. That's a good bet.

BRENDAN. Yeah, but . . . My aspidistras, you know . . .?

JOE. That's a good bet, Bren.

RONNIE. That *is* a good bet.

BRENDAN. . . . They're my pride and joy.

RONNIE. A cigarette versus an aspidistra.

BRENDAN. What the hell do you want with my aspidistras?

RONNIE. I like them.

BRENDAN. You like them.

RONNIE. I've seen them over the back wall. They're gorgeous.

BRENDAN (*pause*). Two cigarettes versus one aspidistra.

RONNIE. Two?!

BRENDAN. Two. I'm not going any lower.

JOE. You'd better hurry. (*Pause.*)

RONNIE (*to* BRENDAN). All right.

JOE (*looking at watch*). You'd better hurry, lads.

BRENDAN. All right. (*To* RONNIE.) We'll just play one hand, without sees and bluffs and stuff. Just the . . . We pick up and then we show our hands. Make it quicker, all right?

JOE. That's not poker.

BRENDAN. It's just a short wager.

JOE. That's not how you play the game.

BRENDAN. We haven't got time to play a proper game. I haven't got the nerves. (*To* RONNIE.) Right, Ronnie?

RONNIE. Right.

BRENDAN *and* RONNIE *sit down at the table.* BRENDAN *picks up the deck of cards.*

JOE. You're prostituting the art, you fool. You're bastardising it. You don't bastardise the skill and the art.

BRENDAN (*ignoring him*). Okay. Aspidistra versus cigarettes. Two cigarettes. Let's go. You shuffle, Joe?

JOE. I'm not going to aid in the tainting of those cards.

BRENDAN. You want to shuffle, Ronnie?

RONNIE. All right.

RONNIE *shuffles and deals.*

BRENDAN (*looking at hand*). Okay. Gimme . . . Gimme . . . What do you want?

RONNIE. What do *you* want?

BRENDAN. Gimme three.

BRENDAN *throws down three and* RONNIE *gives him three from the deck.*

RONNIE. Three. And I'll have . . . two.

He throws down two and takes two from the deck.

All right?

BRENDAN. Yep.

RONNIE. What have you got?

BRENDAN. What have *you* got?

RONNIE. You go. Show me your hand.

BRENDAN. You first.

RONNIE. Dealer has choice, Brendan. Go.

BRENDAN. What choice? Dealer goes first.

RONNIE. Dealer doesn't go first.

BRENDAN. Dealer goes first.

RONNIE. Dealer *says* who goes first.

BRENDAN. Joe. What's the rule?

JOE. You *broke* all the rules.

BRENDAN. Who shows their hand first?

RONNIE. Dealer has choice. And it doesn't matter anyway.

JOE. Congratulations, lads. Anarchy. Anarchy in poker.

BRENDAN (*to* JOE). Who shows first?

RONNIE. It doesn't matter a whit, Brendan.

BRENDAN. It doesn't matter?

RONNIE. Not a whit.

BRENDAN. Well, it matters to me. You show.

   RONNIE *sighs. Then lays down his cards.*

RONNIE. Three Jacks.

BRENDAN (*laying down cards*). Balls! Two sixes.

RONNIE. One aspidistra, s'il vous plait. (*Pause.*)

BRENDAN. Another hand.

RONNIE. That's it. No, no. That's it. One hand. We played it
   and I won. I'm sorry for your loss.

BRENDAN. Fuck off.

RONNIE. No, I am. (*Pause.*) I know how much they mean to you.

BRENDAN. Yeah, well . . .

RONNIE. And I'll take good care of them.

BRENDAN. I hope so. It.

RONNIE. Sorry. It.

JOE. Hundreds of years of tradition and ancestry, destroyed over bloody cigarettes.

RONNIE. And the plant, Joe.

JOE. Yeah. And a bloody plant.

RONNIE (*to* BRENDAN). An extremely well cultivated plant.

BRENDAN. Thanks.

JOE. You shouldn't be allowed to play if you can't show deference or respect to the game.

The telephone rings. JOE *jumps up and answers it.*

(*Into phone.*) Hello? (*Pause.*) Yes, he's . . . Is this important? (*Pause.*) No, no, no, I'm not being . . . I thought I already told you that . . . All right, right, right, here he is. Yes. I'm sorry. Here you go.

JOE *holds the receiver out to* RONNIE. RONNIE *takes it from him.* JOE *sits back down.*

RONNIE (*into phone*). Yes? Yes, I'm here. No, nothing's . . . Everything's . . . (*Pause.*) He's fine. (*Pause.*) No, they're all . . . It's just us. Yes, I'm . . . (*Pause.*) Yes, I'm doing what I can. Guess what I just did? Just now. I won one of Brendan's aspidistras off him. Yep. I . . . (*Pause.*) Yes, you . . . Okay, I will. Yes, I will. *Now.* Okay. (*Pause.*) Right, byebye. I lo . . . I love you too. Yes, that much. And more. Bye. (*Hangs up.*) Jesus!

BRENDAN. They should be . . .

SONIA *enters.*

SONIA. Who was that?

RONNIE. My . . . bane.

SONIA. Karen again?

RONNIE. The hooer.

BRENDAN. Shouldn't . . .? He's late.

JOE. They're both late. (*Pause.*)

SONIA. Who won?

BRENDAN. He did.

SONIA. Well done, Ronnie.

RONNIE. Yeah. Listen, Brendan.

BRENDAN. What?

RONNIE. She says I have to see it.

BRENDAN. See what?

RONNIE. My aspidistra.

BRENDAN. Now?

RONNIE. Yeah.

BRENDAN (*getting up*). Jesus.

JOE (*looking at watch*). You'd better hurry, Bren.

BRENDAN. Right. Right.

  BRENDAN *goes out the door to the kitchen.*

RONNIE. Sure he's loads anyway, hasn't he?

JOE. He does, Ronnie. You won it fair and square.

  We hear the back door open.

BRENDAN (*off-stage*). Sonia!

SONIA. What?

BRENDAN. The fucking dog! For fuck . . .!

SONIA. You let it in, Bren. If you let it in, you've to put it out.

BRENDAN. I'm trying to do . . . For fff . . .!

We hear a scuffle. Then the back door opens and closes.
BRENDAN *re-enters with an aspidistra.*

SONIA (*to* BRENDAN). All right?

RONNIE. Oh, my God.

BRENDAN (*giving aspidistra to* RONNIE). There you go.

RONNIE. Oh, Jaysus. Thanks very much, Brendan.

BRENDAN. Now, do you know how to take care of it?

RONNIE. Oh, I do. I do. It's a beauty.

BRENDAN (*to* SONIA). Bloody mutt.

SONIA. She's not a mutt.

RONNIE (*of aspidistra*). And it's mine, you know?

BRENDAN. That was the best one.

RONNIE. I don't believe you, Brendan, and I don't care. It's
gorgeous.

BRENDAN. Good.

SONIA (*Pause. To* BRENDAN). Should we not leave that
phone off the hook?

RONNIE. Good idea. If she's going to ring again, I don't want
to talk to her.

BRENDAN. No. What if . . .? In case the Drongo or the Crazy
Horse rings.

SONIA. No. Yeah. You're right.

RONNIE (*admiring his aspidistra*). Still . . .

BRENDAN. Leave it the way it is.

SONIA. You're right. Yeah. (*Pause.*)

JOE. Thing about phones. Interesting . . .

They are interrupted by a loud knocking on the door.
Everybody is silent. Expectant.

Lights down.

Lights up.

Moments later. All present with one addition. THE
DRONGO. *A powerful, dangerous looking character. He
sits in the antique armchair like a king and speaks with a
strong Australian accent.* RONNIE*'s aspidistra sits on the
coffee table.*

DRONGO. Not on your nellie. Not. On. Your. Nellie. I came
here . . . And I can see that you're not bad people. Fair
dinkum. But I can see you're not fighting to keep your
heads above water either. I came here alone as opposed to
sending some of my mates, because I wanted to see for
myself what kind of a situation we have. Now, maybe
Raymond Murphy was a good man. He *was* a good man.
Personally, I don't think this business is the *right* business
for a good man. And I believe that that's the essential reason
he failed in this business. Perhaps the next . . . Who knows?
Now, he might have been the type of bloke you could go up
to and say, 'Sorry mate. Bit short today. Next week?' And
he'd say, 'No problems.' But, therein I believe to be the
genesis of his insolvency; his downfall. He was too bloody
nice. Well, now I own your debt. And I'm sorry, but I can't
allow . . . My good business sense, my instinct for survival
tells me I can't allow . . . can't offer leniency in payments.
Regarding neither time nor amount. I can't allow it. (*Pause.*)

SONIA. We have . . . We . . .

DRONGO. Wait, now. Just wait a minute. I'm not finished
talking yet. When I finish talking, then we can all talk. All
right?

SONIA. All right.

DRONGO. Don't interrupt me again.

SONIA. I'm sorry. (*Pause.*)

DRONGO. Do you . . . About leniency. Have you understood
what I just said?

SONIA. Yes.

BRENDAN. Yes.

DRONGO. Good. Now, I'm sure you've heard certain stories
about me. Certain myths or legends . . . Urban legends
which have been passed around in one way or another.
Things I did or threatened to do. Horror stories? Let me tell
you, mates . . . They're all true. I collect on time always.
I collect or I do something. I don't have a set rule for
punishment or *prompting*. Like that term, prompting?
Prompting. A prompter. To prompt. I don't have a set rule.
I just do whatever comes into my head at the time. It's been
said I have a good imagination. I collect or I do something.
Remember that. Now, I came here alone as a gesture of . . .
not goodwill, 'cos I don't have any. As a gesture of trust.
If you have any thoughts on getting out of this not corres-
ponding to my rules, dismiss them now. If something should
ever happen to me, you will be found and killed. Did I just
say killed? You're damn right I did. This was just a little
chat to . . . set forward, to give you a little knowledge of the
situation. Do you understand?

BRENDAN. Yes.

SONIA. Yes.

DRONGO. Now, we'll discuss how to *deal* with the situation.
(*Indicates* JOE.) Who's this?

BRENDAN. My brother.

DRONGO. Don't see much resemblance there. Same father?

BRENDAN. Yes.

DRONGO. Mother?

BRENDAN. Yes.

DRONGO. Hmm. (*Indicates* RONNIE.) And this?

BRENDAN. That's Ronnie. Next door neighbour.

DRONGO. And what's he doing here?

BRENDAN. We were playing cards.

DRONGO. Yeah? Who won?

BRENDAN. He did.

DRONGO (*to* RONNIE). How much did you win?

RONNIE. I won an aspidistra.

DRONGO. A what?

RONNIE (*points at aspidistra*). There.

DRONGO. Yeah, yeah. I know what it is. Beautiful species. Beautiful. Sad to lose it, Brendan?

BRENDAN. Yeah.

DRONGO. High bloody stakes.

BRENDAN (*gloomily*). Yeah.

RONNIE (*simultaneously/happily*). Yeah.

DRONGO. Not much luck tonight, Brendan?

BRENDAN. Not much.

DRONGO. And this is your lovely Sheila. (*To* SONIA.) What's your name?

SONIA. Sonia.

DRONGO. Nice. You could almost *be* a Sheila.

SONIA. Eh . . . Thanks.

DRONGO. A *lovely* looking Sheila.

SONIA. Thank you.

DRONGO. All right. Now that we all know each other, let's get down to business. You owed Mr Murphy, and now me, six hundred and fifty pounds to be repaid at a rate of seventy pounds per week?

BRENDAN. That's right.

DRONGO. One hundred pounds a week now. All right? It's nicer to round these things off, I think. Seventy pounds. That's a disgustingly *odd* amount. One hundred pounds a week?

BRENDAN. Eh . . .

DRONGO. A nice figure?

BRENDAN. Yeah.

DRONGO. All right. Now. Since Mr Murphy went out of business, so to speak, you've missed a week's payment . . .

SONIA. That's . . . But . . .

DRONGO. . . . through, settle down, through no fault of your own. I understand. That's all Mr Murphy's fault. I'm not blaming you. But you know that you now owe me two hundred pounds. Is that right? That's the correct figure? (*Pause.*)

SONIA. We don't have it.

DRONGO (*to* SONIA). Excuse me. (*To* BRENDAN.) What?

BRENDAN. We don't have it.

DRONGO. The money.

BRENDAN. Yes.

DRONGO. At all.

BRENDAN. We have . . . How much? Sixty five pounds. (*Pause.*)

DRONGO. That's not much.

BRENDAN. No.

DRONGO (*to* JOE *and* RONNIE). What about you? None of you any?

JOE. That includes what I added.

SONIA. We weren't given any time.

DRONGO. You poor people. You poor people. (*Pause.*) Hmm.

BRENDAN. Could we not . . .

DRONGO. No. No. I'm sorry.

BRENDAN. No chance of a . . .

DRONGO. . . . No.

BRENDAN. . . . of an extension? A few days or . . .?

DRONGO. I'm sorry, Brendan.

BRENDAN (*short pause*). At all?

DRONGO (*pause*). At all. (*Pause.*)

BRENDAN. We don't have it. I . . . Ronnie!

DRONGO. Ronnie?

RONNIE. No.

BRENDAN. At all?

RONNIE. I'm as smashed as you are. I've got . . . (*Roots in his pocket and takes out some money.*) . . . twelve pounds fifty. Here.

BRENDAN. No, it's all right.

RONNIE. Go ahead. I'll manage.

BRENDAN. No, keep it.

RONNIE. No. Go on. Don't worry.

BRENDAN. It won't make any difference.

DRONGO. That's right.

SONIA. Couldn't we . . . Is there no other way to . . . that we could, like . . . Something here.

BRENDAN. Something here?

SONIA. Here. Like the television or . . .

BRENDAN. The telly?

SONIA. Yes.

BRENDAN. I *need* the telly.

DRONGO. I think there are certain things you should be more concerned about at this moment, than watching football, Brendan. (*Pause.*)

BRENDAN. Will you take it?

DRONGO. No.

BRENDAN. Well is there . . .?

DRONGO (*interrupting*). I deal in cash, mates. I'm not in the flogging business. Now, I appreciate your telly's *worth*. But I'm not going to waste my time. (*Pause.*)

SONIA. We've got that chair you're . . .

BRENDAN. Sonia!

SONIA. That chair you're sitting in is worth thousands of pounds. We'll give you that.

BRENDAN. *Cash*, Sonia.

SONIA. You'll get . . . If you sell it, you'll get over five times what we owe you. Well, not five, but close enough. Surely it'd be worth the hassle to . . .

DRONGO (*interrupting*). And would that be fair on you?

SONIA. . . . over two thousand pounds. (*Pause.*)

DRONGO. And would that be fair on you?

SONIA. We don't mind.

DRONGO. But I do. I'm not having that on my conscience. 'Preciate the offer. Cash. (*Pause.*) Cash, cash, cash. You don't have it.

BRENDAN. No.

SONIA. I can't understand why you . . .

DRONGO (*interrupting*). Shut up. (*Pause. To* BRENDAN.) You don't have it.

BRENDAN. No. We've got sixty five pounds.

RONNIE. Seventy seven. Seventy seven fifty if it makes any difference.

DRONGO. It doesn't, mate. Keep it. (*Sighs.*) This is what happens. (*Pause.*) You see, mates, we've got rules here. Rules are what keep society in shape, keep it from getting flabby. Rules are what prevent anarchy. Rules are are the only thing preventing the extinction of the wallaby. Life is rules and rules are what sustain the eh . . . (*Pause.*) And what are we if we break them? Hm? Who are we *to* break them? Nobody. What are we worth *if* we break them? Nothing. We are people without laws and without a code. We're animals.

JOE. That's right.

DRONGO. What?

JOE. A code.

DRONGO. That's right. (*To* BRENDAN.) We are without a code. Without moral values, ethics, eti*quette*, principles, we are without rules. I have to do my job. I have to do my job and I'm sorry, mates. I'm sorry for you. But if I don't stick to my rules, then what am I? (*Pause.*) Does your phone work?

BRENDAN. Em . . .

DRONGO. Your phone.

BRENDAN. Y . . . Yes.

SONIA. Who are you calling?

DRONGO. The prompters.

SONIA. Surely there's . . . Bren!

BRENDAN. Surely there's . . .

DRONGO. Shut up.

The DRONGO *goes to the phone. Before he reaches it, it rings. He picks it up.*

(*Into phone.*) Hello? (*Pause.*) Yes. Yes it is. Would, would, would you mind, please? Ron? Yes, he's fine. Would you mind . . . Would you mind fucking off please? (*Pause.*) Yes, thank you. Stay off the line, please.

He hangs up and begins dialling.

DRONGO. Your sheila, Ronnie.

RONNIE. So I gathered.

SONIA. Bren!

DRONGO. Sounds like a bit of a cunt.

SONIA. Joe!

RONNIE. She's a hooer.

DRONGO (*into phone*). Hello? Yeah. It's the Drongo. The job. What do you think? (*Pause.*) Nice people, yeah. No, nice. (*Pause.*) Really? Strewth! Ed and Mannix there? Good. Bring 'em. (*Pause.*) If you . . . Yeah, if you want. (*Pause.*) Hang on. (*Takes a note book from his pocket. Opens it. Reads.*) 10 Oak Lawns.

SONIA (*becoming more and more terrified*). Bre . . . Joe!

DRONGO (*into phone*). Te . . . In Springfield, you dafty.

SONIA. Joe, for God's sake!

DRONGO (*into phone*). Yes. Okay. See you in a while. Hurry up. (*Hangs up.*)

SONIA (*hysterically*). Joe! Where's the Crazy Horse?!!

There is a knock on the door. Everybody falls silent. Seconds pass.

DRONGO. Get it, Sheila. Sonia.

SONIA *goes out to the front door while everybody else sits in suspense. She returns with the* CRAZY HORSE *leading the way. He is carrying a bag on his shoulder. He practically saunters into the room.*

CRAZY HORSE. Who's the bloke? (*To* RONNIE.) You the bloke?

RONNIE. No.

CRAZY HORSE. Who then? (*To* JOE.) Heya, Joe.

JOE. How's it going?

CRAZY HORSE. Good. Very good. Who is it?

JOE *points out the* DRONGO.

CRAZY HORSE. This is the Drongo.

DRONGO. That's right.

CRAZY HORSE. This. Is. The. Drongo.

DRONGO. Who the fuck are you, mate?

CRAZY HORSE. So. This. Is. The. Famous. Drongo.

DRONGO. Brendan.

CRAZY HORSE. Know who I am?

DRONGO. I just asked you.

CRAZY HORSE. Know who I am?

DRONGO. *Who* the fuck are you?

CRAZY HORSE. I am Lucifer incarnate. I am the Crazy Horse. (*Pause.*)

DRONGO. Know who I am?

CRAZY HORSE. Someone who just messed with the wrong people.

DRONGO. But, do you know who I am?

CRAZY HORSE. You're the Drongo.

DRONGO. That's right. I am the Drongo.

CRAZY HORSE. Well, I'm the Crazy Horse.

DRONGO. So I see. Go home.

The CRAZY HORSE *takes a pistol from his bag and sits down in a vacant armchair, facing the* DRONGO.

CRAZY HORSE. I'm staying here. (*Pause.*)

DRONGO. What do you want?

CRAZY HORSE. Have you ever heard of me?

DRONGO. I've heard vague rumours.

CRAZY HORSE. So you know my reputation.

DRONGO. I've heard rumours, I said.

CRAZY HORSE. Well, they're all true.

DRONGO. Including the one, you have syphillis?

CRAZY HORSE. Very funny. (*Pause.*) I've heard about you.

DRONGO. All true.

CRAZY HORSE. Yeah?

DRONGO. Yeah.

RONNIE. Get on with it.

CRAZY HORSE. What the fff . . . Who's this, Joe?

JOE. The next door neighbour.

DRONGO. Tell him to shut up.

CRAZY HORSE (*to* RONNIE). Shut the fuck up.

BRENDAN. Ronnie.

RONNIE. He's supposed to be doing something.

BRENDAN. He is.

CRAZY HORSE. I am, fuckhole.

JOE. Shut the fuck up, Ronnie.

CRAZY HORSE (*to* DRONGO). So, we both know each other.
We know of one another's . . . reputations.

DRONGO (*impatiently*). Oh, come on. (*To* RONNIE.) No,
Ronnie. I'm sorry. You're right. (*To* CRAZY HORSE.)
Aren't you supposed to be doing something? (*Pause.*)

CRAZY HORSE. These people owe you money.

DRONGO. That's right.

CRAZY HORSE. A load of money.

DRONGO. That's right.

CRAZY HORSE. How much.

DRONGO. Six hundred and fifty pounds.

CRAZY HORSE. Six hundred and fifty pounds.

DRONGO. That's right.

CRAZY HORSE. Well, you can strike it off your whatever.

They don't owe you anything any more.

DRONGO. Is that right?

CRAZY HORSE. That's right. (*Pause.*)

DRONGO. Do you know who you're talking to?

RONNIE. Oh, Jesus.

SONIA. Ronnie, can we get on with this?

DRONGO (*to* CRAZY HORSE). Do you know who . . .? You get in my way and you'll be found. And you're not that hard to find. You'll be found and you'll be . . . DO YOU KNOW WHO THE FUCK YOU'RE TALKING TO?

Suddenly the DRONGO*'s Australian accent sounds very Dublinlike. The angrier he gets, the less Australian he sounds.*

DO YOU KNOW HOW DEEP YOU ARE ALREADY? You're putting your own, and all these people's well being in jeopardy. (*Then: back to Australian accent.*) You're being a . . . a . . . a dingbat! (*Pause.*)

BRENDAN. Maybe eh . . .

CRAZY HORSE. Jesus Christ. Hah! Jesus Christ. You arsehole.

DRONGO. Fuck you.

CRAZY HORSE. You're not . . . Wait a minute. I'm looking and . . . I know who you are.

DRONGO. Drop it, mate.

CRAZY HORSE (*excited*). You have a scar from here to here. (*Indicates elbow to wrist.*) You've got . . . Lemme . . . Where'd you get the teeth?

DRONGO. Excuse me?

CRAZY HORSE. Where'd you get the teeth?

RONNIE. What the hell is he talking about?

CRAZY HORSE (*still to* DRONGO.) Fikey McFarlane.

DRONGO. Who's that?

CRAZY HORSE. That's fucking you. (*Pause.*)

DRONGO. Do I know you?

CRAZY HORSE. Alan Kilby. The fucking showers, man.

DRONGO (*recognising him*). Alan. The sho . . . Shit!

CRAZY HORSE. Where'd you get the accent? I knew it.

DRONGO (*in Dublinese*). It's my . . . Al! It's my whatchamicallit.

CRAZY HORSE. Your gimmick.

DRONGO. My gimmick. How the fuck are you?

CRAZY HORSE. I'm great. Where'd you get the teeth?

DRONGO. Falsers.

CRAZY HORSE. Very nice. *Very* nice.

DRONGO. Not bad. (*Taps teeth with fingertips.*)

CRAZY HORSE. Not bad. Fucking great. Fucking great to see you.

DRONGO. Al!

CRAZY HORSE. Fikey boy! The accent.

DRONGO. My gimmick.

CRAZY HORSE. It slips.

DRONGO. Only if I lose the rag.

CRAZY HORSE. Jesus. How's the dog?

DRONGO. Dead.

CRAZY HORSE. Aww. I'm sorry.

DRONGO. He was never the same after you . . .

Pause. A respectful silence. SONIA *glances at* BRENDAN.

CRAZY HORSE. Sorry about that, too.

DRONGO. Agh! Water under the bridge. You use guns?

CRAZY HORSE (*brandishing his weapon*). Yeah.

DRONGO. Strictly muscle, myself. Can I have a look?

> CRAZY HORSE *hands him the gun. He plays with it.*

> Nice. So, you're on the side of good.

> *He hands back the gun.*

CRAZY HORSE. The meek and indefensible.

DRONGO. Man.

CRAZY HORSE. But not law and order.

DRONGO. Fuck that.

CRAZY HORSE. Fuck the law.

DRONGO. Fucking right. You stayed true. Like the conver . . .
Old times, Al. Shit! The showers!

CRAZY HORSE. The craic!

> *They stand there, facing each other. There is a long pause.*
> *Everybody is silent and confused.*

DRONGO (*full of emotion*). Good to see you, Al.

> *They embrace.*

CRAZY HORSE. Oh, you gobshite, you.

> *They hug for a long time.*

BRENDAN (*to* JOE). This is your . . . weapon?

CRAZY HORSE (*to* DRONGO). You gobshite.

SONIA. What's going on, Joe?

JOE. The intricacies seem to have shifted somewhat here.

CRAZY HORSE (*still hugging the* DRONGO). Those fuckin'
teeth!

> *Lights down.*

> *Lights up.*

> *A few moments later. Everybody sitting.*

DRONGO (*looking at* CRAZY HORSE). Man. (*Pause.*)

CRAZY HORSE. Man.

DRONGO. Oh, man.

CRAZY HORSE. He . . . Joe, he had a fight with this . . . He crashed . . . Where was it? Inchicore. Some gobshite crashed his car into Fikey's and . . .

DRONGO. Al! Al!

CRAZY HORSE. What?

DRONGO. I know you know me as Fikey, but would you call me the Drongo? It's a . . . I've kind of gotten used to it and people, you know? They know me.

CRAZY HORSE. It's your gimmick.

DRONGO. It's my, yeah. I'm the Drongo.

CRAZY HORSE. Then, well, it's only right. We'll call you the Drongo.

DRONGO. Good one.

CRAZY HORSE. And you call me the Crazy Horse.

DRONGO. You want me to.

CRAZY HORSE. Yeah.

DRONGO. 'Cos it's your gimmick too.

CRAZY HORSE. Well, no . . . Yeah. I'm . . . At the moment, I'm trying to establish it as my gimmick. I'm sort of between handles at the moment.

DRONGO. But you're trying to sway to . . .

CRAZY HORSE. Towards my, right, my . . .

DRONGO. Your gimmick.

CRAZY HORSE. . . . My new handle, yeah. I'm in transition.

DRONGO. Right.

CRAZY HORSE. So it's important that people know me as the Crazy Horse . . .

DRONGO. Absolutely.

CRAZY HORSE. . . . and hear the name as often as possible.

DRONGO. Okay. Crazy Horse.

CRAZY HORSE. Okay. So, Joe. This fella crashes into the Drongo, and the poor Drongo smashes his . . . (*To the* DRONGO.) Was it against the steering wheel?

DRONGO (*to* JOE). I wasn't wearing my seatbelt. (*To others.*) Should always wear your seatbelt.

CRAZY HORSE. Right. And knocks his four front teeth out. (*To* DRONGO.) Oh, man, the difference. I'm looking at you. (*To* JOE.) His . . . His . . . (*To* DRONGO.) You were like that for . . . It's difficult to get used to you now.

DRONGO. I suppose the beard too.

CRAZY HORSE. But it's good. It looks good. You look a hell of a lot more handsome now.

DRONGO. I used to think that a fearsome appearance would be more effective. Scare them with . . . (*To* SONIA.) Because I was a state. No teeth here . . . (*Indicates.*) And it was . . .

CRAZY HORSE. It was unattractive.

DRONGO. It wasn't unat*trac*tive. But, for other people it was uncomfortable. So I thought I'd tone it down and offer a more sage, benevolent front. And I thought that in terms of inspiring fear and awe, that it would be . . . (*Pause.*)

CRAZY HORSE. And was it? Is it?

DRONGO. What?

CRAZY HORSE. What you were going to say.

DRONGO. Effective?

CRAZY HORSE. Yeah.

DRONGO. Ask Sonia and Brendan.

CRAZY HORSE (*to* SONIA). Is it?

SONIA. Yes.

DRONGO. You think so?

SONIA. Very.

DRONGO. Thank you. Brendan?

BRENDAN. Effective?

DRONGO. Yes.

BRENDAN. Yes.

DRONGO (*to* CRAZY HORSE). There you go.

CRAZY HORSE. Great. (*Pause.*)

SONIA. Mister . . . Drongo?

DRONGO. Yes?

SONIA. What's the eh . . . What's the, you know? The story?

DRONGO. What do you mean?

SONIA (*pause*). The money.

DRONGO (*dismissively*). It's all right . . .

SONIA. Really?

DRONGO. . . . . It's okay. This is a happy day, so . . .

RONNIE. This is good, now.

CRAZY HORSE (*to* DRONGO). I'm sorry about your dog.

DRONGO. It's all right.

CRAZY HORSE. Do you miss him?

DRONGO. Yeah, I miss him. He was my friend as well as my dog, you know what I mean?

CRAZY HORSE. I'm sorry.

DRONGO. Ah, would you stop. You were some firecracker freak.

CRAZY HORSE. Yeah. It's all guns now. I like the bangs, you know? Did it ever get its hearing back?

DRONGO. No.

CRAZY HORSE. I'm sorry.

DRONGO. That's okay.

CRAZY HORSE. He was a good dog. One of the few.

DRONGO. That's okay.

SONIA (*tentatively. To* CRAZY HORSE). Do you not like dogs?

DRONGO. Fucking hates them.

CRAZY HORSE. With a vengeance.

DRONGO. With a fucking . . . intensity.

CRAZY HORSE. With a rapture. All animals.

DRONGO. You liked Bubbles.

CRAZY HORSE. Bubbles was okay. She was trained well. Didn't go pissing everywhere. I like an animal I'm not afraid to touch for fear of . . . Aaachh! Disgusting.

DRONGO. You didn't get that with Bubbles.

CRAZY HORSE. Bubbles was clean.

DRONGO. Too right. (*Pause.*)

CRAZY HORSE. So, how are things?

DRONGO. In general?

CRAZY HORSE. How's life?

DRONGO. Good. I'm decorating my apartment.

CRAZY HORSE. Where are you living?

DRONGO. In . . . Can't say in front of . . . (*To others.*) Sorry, everyone. You understand. Information is dangerous. (*To* CRAZY HORSE.) We'll drop around later if you want.

CRAZY HORSE. Yeah. I'd love to.

DRONGO. Yeah?

CRAZY HORSE. Yeah.

DRONGO. It's a bit of a mess. I told you. Decorating. Give me your opinion. Or we could go out to eat.

CRAZY HORSE. We'll order something.

DRONGO. Perfect.

CRAZY HORSE. Old times.

DRONGO. Yeah.

CRAZY HORSE. The conversations. And the thing is, in effect, we stayed true to our own realities.

DRONGO. That's right. To our . . . Sure, look at us now. To our principles and our beliefs.

CRAZY HORSE. That's right. (*Pause.*) Man, the conversations. (*To others.*) We used to talk about . . .

DRONGO. Over coffee in Mulligans.

CRAZY HORSE. Man, yeah. Used to talk about how we would do things. We thought we were bohemians.

DRONGO. We *were* bohemians.

CRAZY HORSE. About nonconformity. We would, however way, live outside what was the norm. What was considered the norm, then.

DRONGO. Still is.

CRAZY HORSE. Outside and above the law. 'Course we didn't know then, what our vocations would be.

DRONGO. But, we stayed true.

CRAZY HORSE. To our beliefs. Absolutely.

DRONGO (*pause*). Man. Coffee in Mulligans.

CRAZY HORSE. Coffee and cigarettes.

DRONGO. And poetry.

CRAZY HORSE. Oh, fuck.

DRONGO. And Gauloises.

CRAZY HORSE. Oh, fuck! And Gitanes.

DRONGO. And Serge Gainsbourg.

CRAZY HORSE. Fuck!

DRONGO. Nonconformity. The buzzword of the late seventies.
(*To others.*) See, that's what separates us from you. You're
in prison for all intents and purposes. You don't know what
freedom is. Of course if there weren't people like you, there
wouldn't be people like me.

CRAZY HORSE. Or me.

DRONGO. That's right.

JOE. They say that . . . Just listening to . . .

DRONGO (*to others*). Because you're . . . (*To* JOE.) What?

JOE. They say that . . . Now this isn't me.

CRAZY HORSE. What do they say?

RONNIE. I'm going to just . . . (*Everybody looks at him.*) Just
going up to the loo.

DRONGO. Oh, go on, yeah. Go ahead. Oh, by the . . . (*To*
SONIA.) Sheila.

SONIA. Sonia.

DRONGO. Sonia. Sorry. Could we have some coffee?

SONIA. I don't know if we've . . .

DRONGO (*interrupting. To* CRAZY HORSE). Coffee?

CRAZY HORSE. I'm more a tea man nowadays.

DRONGO. Old times. (*Pause.*)

CRAZY HORSE (*to* SONIA). Give us a coffee.

SONIA. I don't know if we've any.

BRENDAN. There's some in the biscuit press, Sonia. Behind
the . . . At the back.

SONIA. Two coffees. (*Exits.*)

DRONGO (*calling after her*). Black. (*Pause.*)

CRAZY HORSE (*to* JOE). What do they say, Joe?

JOE. Oh, nothing.

CRAZY HORSE. We're interested. Come on.

JOE. Just . . .

DRONGO. Something about the lifestyle?

CRAZY HORSE. Fucking right.

JOE. Yeah.

DRONGO. Well, what?

JOE. They say that . . . Not me, now . . . that people like you . . . You said we were in a prison because we're, I suppose you mean . . . because we obey the law and worry about mortgages and whatever. The children. School and shit. We're in a prison.

DRONGO. Yeah.

JOE. But conscience, they say. Because your actions and what you do . . . (*The* DRONGO *makes to interject.*) Hang on. Conscience. Because what you do is against the law and against the norm and . . . not very nice. Then you're in a prison. The prison of your conscience. Because however free you are, physically, to do stuff, you're bounded by your guilt and your conscience. Say you . . . Say the bloke who crashed you. To get revenge. Whatever it is you do. You hurt him . . .

DRONGO. Pulled his teeth out. (CRAZY HORSE *laughs.*)

JOE. Okay, you . . . What?!!

DRONGO. With a fucking pliers. (CRAZY HORSE *laughs.*)

JOE (*pause*). Jesus.

CRAZY HORSE. Go on, Joe.

JOE (*pause*). Okay, well I think you get the idea. You pull his teeth out. Later, you think to yourself, 'I'm not very nice, 'cos I've hurt someone.' Unconsciously, now. Your conscience forces you to think these things. So, these thoughts become a prison. A different type of prison, but a prison all the same. (*Pause.*)

CRAZY HORSE. Jaysus sake!

JOE. No?

DRONGO. Fucking stupid! If I hurt someone, it's for one of two reasons. One: Revenge. In which case I've done right. Two: My job. In which case I've done right. And *him* . . . Except for what he did to my dog . . .

CRAZY HORSE. Ah, here, now.

DRONGO. I'm messing, man, Jaysus . . .!

CRAZY HORSE. All right.

DRONGO (*to* JOE, *continuing*). . . . he's on the side of law and order.

CRAZY HORSE. Hey!

DRONGO. Sorry, but on the . . . Justice. You fight for justice.

CRAZY HORSE. Right. (*Beat.*) Not the law.

DRONGO. Fuck the law.

CRAZY HORSE. Well . . . (*Pause.*) That's just what somebody once said. I heard it.

RONNIE *re-enters the room and sits down. Silence. The* DRONGO *stands up.*

DRONGO (*to* CRAZY HORSE). Give me a look at that gun.

CRAZY HORSE *gives him the gun. The* DRONGO *points the gun at* JOE.

(*To* JOE.) Are you making judgements?

JOE. No.

DRONGO (*going closer to* JOE). Are you sure?

JOE. Yes. fuck.

BRENDAN. Mister . . . Drongo.

DRONGO (*putting gun to* JOE's *head*). Are you positive?

JOE. Yes!!

BRENDAN. What is he . . . Wh . . . Crazy horse?

CRAZY HORSE. Fikey! Drongo!

DRONGO. I'm only messing. (*Sits down. To* CRAZY HORSE.) That's a great gun. Where did you get it?

CRAZY HORSE. A bloke got it for me in Hamburg.

DRONGO. Could you get me one? (*Gives the gun back to* CRAZY HORSE.)

CRAZY HORSE. You want one?

DRONGO. Yeah.

CRAZY HORSE. I'll get you one.

SONIA *re-enters and does the business of giving out the coffee, etc.*

Coffee. Great. Thanks very much. (SONIA *is pouring his coffee.*) That's okay. (*To* DRONGO.) You seeing anyone?

DRONGO. Like what? Love?

CRAZY HORSE. Yeah.

DRONGO. No.

CRAZY HORSE. No one special?

DRONGO. No. (*Pause.*) You?

CRAZY HORSE (*shakes his head*). It's the life.

DRONGO. Sacrifices.

CRAZY HORSE. Still. How's money?

DRONGO. Good. I'm . . . I told you. I'm decorating my apartment.

CRAZY HORSE. That's right, yeah.

DRONGO. You're definitely coming over.

CRAZY HORSE. Yeah. We'll go over. (*Pause.*)

DRONGO. What about you?

CRAZY HORSE. Money?

DRONGO. Yeah.

CRAZY HORSE. I'm okay. Getting by. I don't always *take* money. Those who *have* it . . .

DRONGO. Right.

CRAZY HORSE. These. Brendan and Sonia, I don't take.

DRONGO. Obviously. Because their problem *is* money.

CRAZY HORSE. Exactly.

DRONGO. I understand. So, you decide between those who must pay, and those you do it for, for . . . (*Pause.*)

CRAZY HORSE. I don't know. Justice?

DRONGO. Justice. (*Pause.*) I just go where the money is.

CRAZY HORSE. I know.

DRONGO. It's my job. It's the career I've chosen and I'm bloody good at it.

CRAZY HORSE. I don't doubt it.

DRONGO. But, you. Man, who would have . . . You're the Lone Ranger.

CRAZY HORSE. I was actually going to call myself the Lone *Wolf.*

DRONGO. Not bad. Why didn't you?

CRAZY HORSE. Crazy Horse is better. Has more punch.

DRONGO. That it does. And you get the old Neil Young connection as well.

CRAZY HORSE. Mm. (*Pause.*) Oh, that's right.

DRONGO. Yeah. You smoking these days?

CRAZY HORSE. No. Not in a while.

DRONGO. Me neither. (*Pause.*)

CRAZY HORSE. Crazy Horse was his band, wasn't it.

DRONGO. It was, yeah. Will we have one?

CRAZY HORSE. What?

DRONGO. A smoke?

CRAZY HORSE. Why?

DRONGO. For old times' sakes.

CRAZY HORSE (*short pause*). As a nod to the old days?

DRONGO. Yeah.

CRAZY HORSE. All right.

DRONGO. Anyone got a cigarette? Brendan?

BRENDAN. No.

CRAZY HORSE. Got a cigarette, Joe?

JOE. I've none. Ronnie?

RONNIE. No, I've . . . (*Pause.*) Two, is it?

CRAZY HORSE. Yeah.

> RONNIE *gives them each a cigarette and a light. They sit and smoke.*

DRONGO. Man, the law.

CRAZY HORSE. People. These people.

DRONGO. Fuck them.

CRAZY HORSE. They don't know, do they.

DRONGO. They *don't* know. They worry and they fret.

CRAZY HORSE. And they'll never know.

DRONGO. No.

CRAZY HORSE. It takes a certain type of person.

DRONGO. It does. Someone who'll question things.

CRAZY HORSE. That's it. To question.

DRONGO. To question.

CRAZY HORSE. To question everything.

DRONGO. Exactly.

CRAZY HORSE. To say, 'No. This is wrong, this doesn't suit me and I refuse to obey, to conform, to . . . to . . . '

DRONGO. To do what they want.

CRAZY HORSE. They, yes, they. I'm gonna be me. In myself.

DRONGO. As a . . . *As* myself.

CRAZY HORSE. As . . . *S*omething separate.

DRONGO. As a human.

CRAZY HORSE. A man alone.

DRONGO. As a being.

CRAZY HORSE. As something *of* itself.

DRONGO. A rock.

CRAZY HORSE. As an island. An island *unto* itself.

DRONGO. An island in the stream.

CRAZY HORSE. Precisely. Oh, man. The days.

DRONGO. We're violent? We use violent means? So be it.

CRAZY HORSE. So be it.

DRONGO. Does it shame us?

CRAZY HORSE. 'Course not.

DRONGO. Violence is there, is within us. It's inherent . . .

CRAZY HORSE. That's right.

DRONGO. . . . From birth. We're pulled from the womb, kicking and screaming, aren't we . . .?

CRAZY HORSE. Yep.

DRONGO. Light dazzles us, blood flies . . .

CRAZY HORSE. I remember this. . . . Our arse is smacked.

DRONGO. We play on man's most primordial emotion.

CRAZY HORSE. Fear.

DRONGO. Fear. And therein lies our power.

CRAZY HORSE. Our power, yes. (*Pause.*) Therein it lies. (*Pause.*) Yeah. (*Pause.*)

SONIA. How's the coffee?

DRONGO. Good. Good. Very good.

CRAZY HORSE. Thank you, Sonia.

SONIA. You're welcome. (*Pause.*)

CRAZY HORSE. Do you think . . .? No.

DRONGO. What?

CRAZY HORSE. I forgot that band was called Crazy Horse, now.

DRONGO. So? (*Pause.*) Ah, fuck that.

CRAZY HORSE. . . . You know?, but the name's . . .

DRONGO. Doesn't count, man. Are you a band?

CRAZY HORSE. No.

DRONGO. No, you're a bloke. Different context. D'you get me?

CRAZY HORSE. Suppose.

DRONGO. If you were a band . . .

CRAZY HORSE. I get you. (*Pause.*) That's a nice chair.

DRONGO. Which? This?

DRONGO *looks at chair without getting out of it.*

JOE. That's a horrible chair.

CRAZY HORSE. I like it. Is it old?

SONIA. Over a hundred years.

BRENDAN. It was her grandmother's.

CRAZY HORSE. It's nice.

RONNIE. I'd better go.

CRAZY HORSE. Where are you going?

RONNIE. The wife.

CRAZY HORSE. Fuck the wife. She run your life?

RONNIE. Well, actually she does, the hooer.

CRAZY HORSE. Fuck her. Hang around. You're good company.

DRONGO. That was her ringing earlier.

CRAZY HORSE. That was . . .? (*To* RONNIE.) Where do you live?

RONNIE. Next door.

CRAZY HORSE. And she's ringing?!

DRONGO. He doesn't like her.

CRAZY HORSE (*to* RONNIE). No?

RONNIE. Well . . .

CRAZY HORSE. Fuck her. Man. That is some fine chair. What do you think, Drongo?

The DRONGO *stands up and has a look at the chair.*

How would that look in your apartment?

DRONGO. It would . . . Jesus, actually . . . That's a nice chair.

BRENDAN. It's an eyesore.

DRONGO. Shut up. That's a . . . That's a fucking antique. That's a nice chair. (*Pause. Still looking at chair.*) I'll tell you what . . . (*To* CRAZY HORSE.) What do you think of that chair?

CRAZY HORSE. It's not bad, is it?

DRONGO (*to* BRENDAN). I'll tell you what. I'll take that chair as payment for what you owe me.

BRENDAN. What?

JOE. What?

DRONGO. I'll cancel your entire debt for this chair. (*To* CRAZY HORSE.) This chair would go beautifully with the wallpaper. We got . . . Did I tell you it's got wooden floors? Wooden with big rugs. Got a Persian too. This chair was *made* for my apartment.

SONIA. But you *said*.

DRONGO. Gorgeous.

SONIA. But you *said*.

DRONGO. What did I say?

BRENDAN. Sonia.

SONIA. He said.

DRONGO. What did I say? (*Pause.*)

SONIA. You said the debt was cancelled.

DRONGO. The debt?

SONIA. You said we were all square.

DRONGO. Excuse me . . .

SONIA. You told us.

DRONGO. Excuse me. What did I tell you?

SONIA. I asked you about the money. I said what about the money, and you said the money was okay. We were all square.

DRONGO. No, no . . .

SONIA. You lied.

DRONGO. . . . excuse me, no.

SONIA. You tell us we're all square and . . .

DRONGO. I did not. The money . . .

SONIA. You told me the money was okay.

BRENDAN. Sonia.

SONIA. That's what he said.

DRONGO. Yes. I said the money was *okay* . . .

SONIA. Yeah.

DRONGO. . . . But I didn't say your debt was cancelled. What kind of a businessman would I be if I cancelled your debt. I'd be out of business, like Raymond Murphy.

SONIA. You said.

DRONGO. Now, hold on. It's not my fault you misinterpreted what I said. I can't just cancel. Why would I say that? Why would I put myself six hundred and fifty quid out of pocket? Who'd do that? A fucking eejit would. What I meant was . . . The money is okay for tonight. My mates. My prompters. For tonight, I'll let you off. I'll give you another week or so to come up with the two hundred pounds you owe me *this* week. I'll give you some time.

SONIA. But . . .

DRONGO. What?

SONIA. We can't . . . (*To* BRENDAN.) Bren. We can't. Even with another week. Two hundred pounds. We can't get that amount of money.

BRENDAN (*to* DRONGO). We can't.

DRONGO. Two hundred pounds.

BRENDAN. We can't.

DRONGO (*sighs*). Do you know what I am? I'm a loan shark. It's my job to collect what I'm owed. I use muscle. (*Pause. Looks at watch.*) I'm a violent man. But I've just met someone I haven't seen in a long time and I'm in a good mood. I'm giving you a chance. A chance you wouldn't have if it wasn't for my joy. The chair for the debt. That's a bargain. What the hell could you want with it? It doesn't match with anything in this room. In *my* apartment . . .

BRENDAN. It's worth a lot of money.

DRONGO. How much?

BRENDAN. Over two thousand pounds.

DRONGO. Really?

RONNIE. That thing? (*Pause. The* DRONGO *stares at him.*)

DRONGO. That's a nice fucking chair.

RONNIE. Why don't you give it to him? That's what you were
    going to do in the first place. It's horrible.

SONIA. No.

BRENDAN. What?

RONNIE. Why the sudden change? That was what you were . . .

SONIA. He lied.

DRONGO. I told you.

SONIA. No. You led us to believe something that wasn't the
    truth. You said okay. (*To* BRENDAN.) He said we were all
    square. (*To* DRONGO.) We can't let you have this chair.
    You changed the rules.

DRONGO. I didn't change any rules.

SONIA. You did. You changed the rules. You said okay. When
    I asked you about the money, that's what you said.

DRONGO. You misinterpreted me.

SONIA (*to* BRENDAN). He does not get that chair.

BRENDAN. Sonia.

SONIA. No. No.

DRONGO. Sonia. Think about this. I don't get this chair,
    something bad is going to happen to you. You just told me
    you can't get the money. I have to do my job. I'm offering
    you a way out. (*Pause.*) You don't want to be prompted.

JOE (*to* CRAZY HORSE). What do you think? (*Pause.*) Al.

CRAZY HORSE. Crazy Horse.

JOE. Crazy Horse. What do you think?

CRAZY HORSE. He's right. She misinterpreted.

SONIA. I did not.

JOE. Did you forget why you're here?

CRAZY HORSE. The Drongo's my friend.

DRONGO. Buds, huh?

CRAZY HORSE. . . . We're the buds.

JOE. But, did you forget why you're here?

CRAZY HORSE. The Drongo is my friend. (*Pause.*)

JOE. You've no ethics.

CRAZY HORSE. Yes I do.

JOE. You're the one who lied. You were supposed to protect us. We asked you. There are no ethics there. You've no code.

DRONGO (*to* SONIA). That's a great chair. I like that chair. You don't even like it.

SONIA. That's not the point.

DRONGO. I'm taking it off your hands.

SONIA. That's not the point.

DRONGO. The fucking point?

SONIA. You said we were all square. (*Pause.*)

DRONGO. Jesus, these fucking people. (*Pause. Sighs.*) All right. I'll tell you what. I'm in a good mood. You're lucky. Here's an idea. I'll play a hand of poker with Brendan. We'll play one hand of poker. If he wins, and because of our misunderstanding, I'll absolve all debts and you can keep the chair. How's that sound?

SONIA. No. No way. We're in enough debt, Brendan. Don't start gambling what we . . .

DRONGO. No, no, no, no, wait a minute, wait a minute. This is the . . . You'll like this part. If *I* win, all right? If *I* win, I get the chair *and* I absolve all debts. See? So, whether you win or lose, your debt is still cancelled. You win simply by playing. You've nothing to lose except the chair, which you don't like anyway.

JOE. That sounds fair.

DRONGO. A better deal in this life, you'll never see. (*Pause.*)

JOE. That's a good bet.

RONNIE. It is.

DRONGO. Well?

BRENDAN. I like it. Sonia, come on.

SONIA. How do we know he'll keep his word?

BRENDAN. He will.

SONIA. But how do we know?

BRENDAN. Sonia, will you stop making things difficult. He will.

DRONGO. There's just one more thing. Because the deal is so good, I want one thing extra.

SONIA. I knew it. You see?

BRENDAN. Sonia, come on.

DRONGO. Just a small thing. It's still a great deal.

SONIA. I knew it.

BRENDAN. Sonia. (*To* DRONGO.) What is it?

DRONGO. If I win, I also get an aspidistra.

SONIA. Oh. Fair enough.

BRENDAN. Ah, now, hold on a sec.

SONIA. Come on, Bren.

BRENDAN. I already lost one of my aspidistras to Ronnie.

SONIA. You've loads.

DRONGO. It's still a great deal. (*Pause.*)

BRENDAN. All right. One . . .

DRONGO. Just one.

BRENDAN. . . . . Fuck sake! (*Short pause.*) All right. Let's play.

DRONGO. Would you mind bringing my one in first? Can I see one?

BRENDAN. Why?

DRONGO. Just to see if they're any good.

BRENDAN. They *are* good. They're the best of aspidistras. (*Pointing to* RONNIE'*s.*) Sure, there.

DRONGO. I don't doubt your gardening skills, Brendan. I'd just like to see what I'm playing for.

BRENDAN (*sighs*). Sonia? Will you . . .?

SONIA. Yeah. (SONIA *exits.*)

DRONGO. Okay, then. Lets get started here.

Pebbles the dog runs into the sitting room and behind the sofa with SONIA *in hot pursuit.*

SONIA. Pebbles!

BRENDAN. Sonia, the fucking dog. (*To everybody.*) Watch this. Watch. In behind the sofa. Straight in. Behind the sofa. Pisses. (*To* SONIA.) Sonia, the fucking dog. (*To others.*) Pisses. Every time he's let in. Why? Because he was never trained properly. I put his nose in it and give him a clatter, but what does she do? She pets him and cuddles him. Look.

SONIA *has picked the dog up and is doing just that.*

Put his nose in it.

SONIA. Leave him alone.

BRENDAN. So he doesn't learn. It'd only take a couple of days to teach him, but with her cuddling him, he just gets confused. He doesn't know, so he pisses out of confusion.

CRAZY HORSE (*contemptuously*). That's disgusting.

BRENDAN (*pointing behind sofa*). Look at that, Sonia.

SONIA. Wait. (*She exits with the dog.*)

CRAZY HORSE. I wouldn't put up with that, Brendan.

BRENDAN. What can I do? It's her dog.

CRAZY HORSE. Want me to put it out of its misery?

BRENDAN. No, no.

DRONGO. Put it out of its misery.

BRENDAN. No, please, Jesus. It's Sonia's dog. If it was mine, you know . . .?

DRONGO. Come on . . .

BRENDAN. . . . be a *different* story, but . . .

DRONGO. . . . . Are we playing cards or what?

CRAZY HORSE (*to* DRONGO). Did you see what that dog did?

DRONGO. Yeah.

CRAZY HORSE. I wouldn't have it, Brendan.

BRENDAN. It has some good qualities. It's not all bad.

SONIA *re-enters with the aspidistra. She hands it to the* DRONGO.

SONIA. Here we go.

DRONGO (*examining it*). Oh, that's nice. That'll . . . (*To* CRAZY HORSE.) What do you think?

CRAZY HORSE. Lovely.

DRONGO (*to himself*). That'll look great. Oh, yeah.

RONNIE *picks his aspidistra up and sits cradling it until stated.*

BRENDAN. That was the best one.

DRONGO. I'd believe it, Brendan. I'd believe it. (*Pause.*) All right. Let's play.

BRENDAN *and the* DRONGO *sit down at the table. Everybody else moves closer to watch the game. The cards are taken out.*

BRENDAN. Okay. Ooookay. Debt versus chair and one aspidistra. (*To* DRONGO.) You want to deal?

DRONGO. I don't mind.

BRENDAN. Okay, I'll deal. (*Shuffles cards.*)

DRONGO. Why doesn't someone who's not playing deal?

BRENDAN. All right. Joe?

CRAZY HORSE. I'll deal.

The CRAZY HORSE *takes the cards and deals them expertly. Each player looks at his hand. Pause.*

DRONGO. I'll have three.

BRENDAN. I'll have three, too.

They throw down and the CRAZY HORSE *deals them out three cards each.*

DRONGO. Okay, I'll . . . Who sees first? I'll see you.

BRENDAN. Can you do that? (*To* JOE.) Who sees first, Joe?

JOE. It doesn't matter.

DRONGO. *Course* it matters.

JOE. It doesn't. It doesn't make any difference who sees who first. The bets are set. The only difference it makes is who sees first, which doesn't make any difference. If you were in Vegas, it would, because you'd be upping the bet all the time and bluffing and all. Here's there's none of that. There's no tactics involved, so you're just seeing.

DRONGO. All right. (*Pause.*) Who goes first?

BRENDAN. You.

DRONGO. No, you.

SONIA. Go, Bren.

BRENDAN sighs. Pause. He lays down his cards.

BRENDAN. Three fives.

The DRONGO *lays down his cards.*

DRONGO. Two aces.

BRENDAN (*pause*). I win.

DRONGO. What?

BRENDAN. The debt is cancelled. (*Unsure.*) Am I right?

SONIA. And we keep the chair.

BRENDAN. *And* the plant.

RONNIE (*cradling his aspidistra*). One of them.

DRONGO. I had two aces.

BRENDAN. Three fives beats it.

DRONGO. But I have aces.

BRENDAN. It doesn't matter. Three of anything beats two of anything.

JOE. He's right.

DRONGO. Even aces?

BRENDAN. Even aces.

DRONGO (*to* CRAZY HORSE). Does it?

CRAZY HORSE. 'Fraid so. (*Pause.*)

DRONGO. Fuck.

SONIA. So our debt is cancelled.

DRONGO (*of cards*). Are you sure?

SONIA. Mr Drongo?

DRONGO. What?

SONIA. Our debt is cancelled?!

DRONGO (*pause. To* BRENDAN). I'll play you again.

JOE. Play him again?

DRONGO. Two out of three.

JOE. What?

SONIA. I told you, Brendan.

DRONGO. That was just a warmer upper . . .

SONIA. I told you.

DRONGO. . . . get me going.

SONIA. I told you something like this would happen.

JOE. What's he . . .?

BRENDAN. I beat you.

JOE. Two out of three?

DRONGO. Two out of three. I wasn't sure of the rules.

JOE. Where has all the chivalry gone?

SONIA (*to* BRENDAN). I knew it.

JOE. . . . The honour.

SONIA. You should have known.

BRENDAN. I beat you fair and square.

DRONGO. Two out of three.

SONIA. Fair and square. That was it. Go away.

DRONGO. Don't you get that way with me, miss. (*To* CRAZY HORSE.) What do you think of that chair?

CRAZY HORSE (*less enthusiastically than before*). It's a nice chair.

DRONGO. It's perfect. (*To* BRENDAN.) I'll play you again.

SONIA. Why don't you go away and leave us alone?

RONNIE. Brendan won, now.

BRENDAN. I beat you.

JOE. He beat you like a gentleman. Don't disgrace yourself, Drongo. This'll look very bad.

DRONGO. Fuck you. I want that chair. I have the power.

JOE. This'll look very bad.

DRONGO. Shut up or you'll be prompted. I've lads coming who'll . . .

The DRONGO *goes over to the window and looks out.*

JOE. You're not staying true to your own reality.

The DRONGO *turns from the window.*

DRONGO. What's the . . . What?!

JOE. Think about it.

DRONGO. What the fuck are you talking about? Two out of three, Brendan.

SONIA. You're not getting that chair. (*To* CRAZY HORSE.) Crazy Horse. You know what's right. (*Pause.*) Crazy Horse!

CRAZY HORSE (*confused*). I don't know.

DRONGO. What do you mean, you don't know? You stick with your friends.

CRAZY HORSE. I *don't* know, man.

JOE. There's a code, am I right?

DRONGO. There is no code . . .

JOE. There is, there's . . .

DRONGO. . . . . I have the power and that's that.

JOE. What's power without a code? Know what I mean?

DRONGO. I don't . . . You're . . .

JOE. What's the sword without Bushido?

DRONGO. . . . . He's talking in riddles.

JOE. You spoke about a code.

The phone rings. The DRONGO, *who is standing next to it, picks it up.*

DRONGO (*into phone*). Fuck off! (*Hangs up.*) Crazy Horse.

JOE. Crazy Horse. You know what's right. (*To* DRONGO.) Do you remember talking about a code?

DRONGO. I don't remember.

SONIA. Crazy Horse.

CRAZY HORSE. What?!!

SONIA. Do something!

CRAZY HORSE. Do something?

JOE. Will you do something!

BRENDAN. Why don't you fucking do something!

DRONGO. I have the power!

The CRAZY HORSE *goes over to the window and looks out.*

They'll be here soon.

RONNIE (*to the* DRONGO). You're only an oul' hooer.

DRONGO. I'm a hooer? Your *wife's* a fuckin' hooer.

SONIA (*to* CRAZY HORSE). Why don't you do something?

CRAZY HORSE (*still looking out the window*). Shut up.

DRONGO. Yeah. Shut up, you slapper. Crazy Horse. Tell them.
    You're the man.

The CRAZY HORSE *turns from the window. To the*
DRONGO.

CRAZY HORSE. What happened to you?

DRONGO. What are you talking about?

CRAZY HORSE. What happened to you? (*Pause.*)

DRONGO. I'm your bud, man.

SONIA. He's not your bud. He's a monster.

DRONGO. My prompters'll be here in a minute.

SONIA. He's nobody's bud.

DRONGO (*to* SONIA). Shut up. (*To* CRAZY HORSE.) We'll
    deal with these fuckers and get some grub.

CRAZY HORSE. I don't know.

JOE. We hired you, you prick.

DRONGO. You don't know?

JOE. Where's your work ethic?

DRONGO. You don't fucking know? Who are you going to side with? Weakness or Power?

CRAZY HORSE (*brandishing gun*). *I* have the power, Fikey. (*Pause.*)

DRONGO. What are you . . . Are you threatening me? You have the power, yeah. You have the power for the moment. I know there's, like, our friendship there, and things are complicated. But fairly soon, I'm telling you . . . I'm telling you all . . . There's going to be a prompting.

CRAZY HORSE. Fikey.

DRONGO. Alan. Our friendship . . .

Silence. The two men stand looking at each other. Eventually, SONIA breaks it.

SONIA. Is someone going to do something?

DRONGO. Ah, I'm sick of this fucking shit. Fuck it. You're all dead.

RONNIE. Crazy Horse!

DRONGO. That's it. Everyone in this house, do you hear me . . .?

SONIA. Will you do something!

DRONGO. No-one's getting out.

JOE. Make a fucking . . .

DRONGO. . . . None of youse.

JOE. . . . a decision, will you?

Tense silence. Everyone looking at the CRAZY HORSE.

CRAZY HORSE. *Am* I a Neil Young rip-off?!!

Suddenly, a car screeches into the driveway. The CRAZY HORSE runs to the window and looks out.

DRONGO. That'll be them, now.

Car lights fill up the room through the window.

SONIA. Brendan.

DRONGO. Youse are all . . .

BRENDAN. Sonia.

BRENDAN *and* SONIA *embrace.*

DRONGO. . . . fucking . . .

The car lights turn off. The CRAZY HORSE *turns from the window with a sudden movement. He slips in the dog's piss. His feet fly out from underneath him an he shoots the* DRONGO *in the chest. The* DRONGO *falls down dead.* SONIA *screams.* RONNIE, *who is now standing, drops his aspidistra. The pot shatters. From outside, we hear car doors closing and muffled voices. Slowly, the* CRAZY HORSE *emerges from behind the sofa. He takes out a second gun. He now has a gun in each hand. He exits towards the kitchen.* SONIA *and* BRENDAN *are still holding each other. we hear the back door opening, a dog barking, a gunshot . . .*

SONIA. Pebbles!

And then, silence. The CRAZY HORSE *re-enters the room. There is a banging on the hall door. He puts his bag on his shoulder.*

You killed my dog.

The CRAZY HORSE *makes to leave the room, but just before doing so, he turns . . .*

CRAZY HORSE. I hate those filthy beasts!

The CRAZY HORSE *exits. We hear the front door opening, followed by shouting, gunfire, and general chaos. Tableau.* RONNIE *stands over his aspidistra.* JOE *sits.* BRENDAN *and* SONIA *hold one another. The telephone begins to ring again.*

Blackout.